To Helen and Lee Lovaas

*It's pretty amazing to watch faithful people use their resources
to make a difference in the world. HomeWord is so fortunate
to have been touched by your kindness and generosity.
You have made a difference!*

JIM BURNS

faith
conversations
for
families

Regal

From Gospel Light
Ventura, California, U.S.A.

Published by Regal
From Gospel Light
Ventura, California, U.S.A.
www.regalbooks.com
Printed in the U.S.A.

Library of Congress Cataloging-in-Publication Data
Burns, Jim, 1953-
Faith conversations for families / Jim Burns.
p. cm.
ISBN 978-0-8307-5869-2
1. Christian education—Home training. 2. Families—Religious life. I. Title.
BV1590.B86 2011
248.8'45—dc22
2010048552

Rights for publishing this book outside the U.S.A. or in non-English languages are
administered by Gospel Light Worldwide, an international not-for-profit ministry.
For additional information, please visit www.glww.org, email info@glww.org, or write
to Gospel Light Worldwide, 1957 Eastman Avenue, Ventura, CA 93003, U.S.A.

To order copies of this book and other Regal products in bulk quantities,
please contact us at 1-800-446-7735.

CONTENTS

Take the Faith Conversations Challenge

The Faith Conversations Challenge is a 52-week experience designed to enhance your family's spiritual growth and form a positive habit of energizing your family's spiritual life for the better. Studies tell us that 80 percent of kids leave the church after high school.[1] However, the chances that they will stay in the church are improved greatly if there are healthy family-time faith conversations in the home.

This book contains ready-to-go spiritual conversation starters for you and your preteen and teenage kids. It has been created to inspire and prompt rich dialog that is relational and spiritually meaningful. The best and most effective learning is seldom from lectures or preaching but from good, healthy sharing and dialog. Each of the 52 chapters offers a practical, biblical basis for your family's spiritual life that will help you grow together and strengthen each person's relationship with God, no matter his or her age. There are levels of spiritual learning that take place at different ages, and we've done our best to make these conversations adaptable for families with children ages 10 and older.

We have divided each chapter into three parts: "Focus," "In the Word" and "Reflect and Apply." The "Focus" is a story or anecdote that draws on the theme of the chapter. "In the Word" is a simple relational Bible study with a practical twist. The "Reflect and Apply" section gives your family a chance to dialog about how the lesson applies to your daily lives.

We have placed more materials in this book than you will probably need; please feel free to adapt this resource to fit your time frame and family needs. The goal is to enjoy conversations about spirituality, to learn together as a family and to develop the habit of a special family time.

The Faith Conversation Challenge is to spend time together as a family 20 minutes a week for 52 weeks—and to make it fun! If you miss a week, don't worry. Just start again the next week. It's the process that counts. You will see the rewards in your family's life for years to come.

Note

1. Drew Dyck, "The Leavers: Young Doubters Exit the Church," *Christianity Today*, November 19, 2010. http://www.christianitytoday.com/ct/2010/november/27.40.html?start=1.

Family-Time Faith-Focused Conversations

There is an extremely exciting and growing movement among people of faith: to bring faith-focused conversations back into the home. As researchers began to bring bad news to Christian families that kids were leaving the church in their late teens and early 20s, another bit of research appeared at the same time that was very good news: *Families where healthy faith-focused conversations took place on a regular basis saw their children remain strong in their faith and involved in their relationship with God.* One of the most common questions we are asked at HomeWord is, "How do I build a spiritual legacy of faith with my family?" Life is complicated, but the answer to that question is not. In homes where there is an intentional family time dedicated to growing together spiritually, kids thrive. It's good for communication, good for everyone's faith and even good for a marriage.

Family-time faith-focused conversations help families grow spiritually together. Spending time together provides an easy avenue for dialog about important subjects many parents want to talk about but feel ill equipped to discuss with their kids. And when conversation topics are intentional, relevant and relational, there is a natural opportunity for families to pray together as well as study God's Word. This book is designed to get your faith-focused conversations up and running so that you can build in a habit of God-centered family time.

A word to church leaders: More and more faith communities are offering people in their congregation resources like this in order to develop a church-wide family faith conversation at home. Our hope is that you will see this material as one ingredient in your efforts to help the families in your church build a legacy of spiritual growth in their homes.

The Biblical Mandate of the *Shema*

Do you know what the most often quoted Scripture of all time is? Many Christians might answer John 3:16 or maybe Psalm 23, but the most often quoted Scripture from the Bible is by far Deuteronomy 6:4-9. Here's why: Every morning and every evening in Orthodox Jewish homes, this Scripture is said aloud. It is recited every Sabbath. It is quoted at deathbeds and at bar mitzvahs. When Jesus was asked to name the most important commandment, He went directly to Deuteronomy. "You will love the LORD your God with all your heart and with all your soul and with all your strength" (v. 5). These verses, called the *Shema*, were likely the first Scripture Jesus ever heard as a child because it was probably said every day in His home.

Shema is a Hebrew word that means "to listen." The verses in the *Shema* are a mandate for Christians to leave a legacy of faith to our children:

> Hear, O Israel: The LORD our God, the LORD is one. Love the LORD your God with all your heart and with all your soul and with all your strength. These commandments that I give you today are to be upon your hearts. Impress them on your children. Talk about them when you sit at home and when you walk along the road, when you lie down and when you get up. Tie them as symbols on your hands and bind them on your foreheads. Write them on the doorframes of your houses and on your gates (Deuteronomy 6:4-9).

These verses teach us three foundational lessons:

1. Loyalty to God
2. Transmission of faith and love to our children
3. Constant mindfulness of God's teachings

Unfortunately we have lost the *Shema* vision in too many of our homes. It's time to regain that vision and the focus it takes to build a spiritual legacy in our families. The *Shema* shows us that faith is passed on when parents live out an authentic, faithful life to God, leading their kids by example. Transmitting faith to growing children is not the job of the church; rather, the church's role is to come alongside families to help them develop strong faith and values that will guide their children to grow up faithfully and then pass their faith along to the next generation.

It is the calling of parents to disciple children toward spiritual maturity. No one has ever said this is an easy task, and it can definitely get messy. Nonetheless, we are called to develop spiritual growth in the lives of our children—and, as the *Shema* tells us, one important way we can do so is to talk with our kids about life with God: "when you sit at home and when you walk along the road, when you lie down and when you get up" . . . in other words, a lot!

If you haven't yet developed a *Shema*-shaped family, that's okay. This book is designed to help. The content you'll find here has been used in my family and in the families of countless people who would say their family faith conversations are seldom perfect, sometimes powerful, but always worth doing.

How to Use This Book

We often say when working with teens and preteens, K.I.S.S.—Keep It Short and Simple. Think about your kids' ages and temperaments, and choose family-time activities that they will look forward to and enjoy. I love this Scripture from 1 Thessalonians 2:8:

> We loved you so much that we were delighted to share with you not only the gospel of God but our lives as well, because you had become so dear to us.

We are instructed by the *Shema* to give our kids the Good News and teaching of God, but also to share our lives together. Create a warm environment and keep away from preaching, lectures and shame. Those tactics didn't work when you were growing up and they don't work now! Also remember that kids support what they help to create, so keep your teens and preteens engaged by allowing them to plan and even lead family activities.

In the past, too many families made their family devotions time intensely serious and in the process lost the joy of working on their spiritual journey together. My suggestion is to keep the conversations moving and connect family times with food or some kind of a fun event. One family I know always makes a run to the local ice cream parlor after their family times. Another family has a ping-pong or Wii tournament after they meet for 20 minutes. The idea is to make family time a meaningful experience, and nobody said it has to be boring or long. Your job is to enhance spiritual growth and help produce family togetherness.

Take a few quiet minutes on your own or with your spouse before your scheduled family time to look over each week's material. As you prayerfully think about your children, select the portions of dialog and Bible study that you believe will have the most meaning for your family. Then start the conversation! Remember, too, that good *conversation* sometimes heads in unexpected directions, especially when kids are involved. Don't be afraid of tangents and rabbit trails, particularly if your children are younger. The point is to invite God into your family's special time together, and to develop a habit of discussing important spiritual matters in a warm, non-threatening atmosphere.

May God richly bless your family as you share together the Words of Life!

faith
conversations
for
families

1

Prayer:
Communication with God

Key Verse
In the morning, O Lord, you hear my voice;
in the morning I lay my requests before you and wait in expectation.

PSALM 5:3

The Big Idea
Communication with God is what prayer is all about.
A consistent prayer life leads to a deeper, more intimate relationship with God.

Focus

Read the following story aloud, and then use the questions to start a faith conversation.

> As far as Regina Hammond is concerned, luck has little to do with it. The 37-year-old flight attendant won $100,000 in a Colorado lottery game on top of $50,000 she won the previous year the same way. And she's not finished yet. Her goal is the $1 million grand prize. Hammond believes that prayer has paved her way to riches. "I pray to God to help me and He answers," she says.[1]

1. How does Regina Hammond's claim make you feel?

2. If prayer works, why don't all lottery players pray and win?

3. Do you think Hammond will win the million dollars? Why or why not?

4. Should people pray to get rich? To win sports events? To be successful? Why or why not?

5. Some people believe that lotteries are sinful. If that's true, why would God answer Hammond's prayers to win?

6. Would you pray to win a lottery? Why or why not?

7. Read each of the following items aloud. Which of these is okay to pray for? Why?

- An *A* on a test
- Lots of money
- Getting a job
- A better complexion
- Winning a game
- New clothes
- Not getting caught disobeying Mom or Dad
- Getting a date
- Losing or gaining weight

In the Word

Now discuss the following questions and get into the Word together:

1. How is prayer different from a face-to-face conversation?

2. Name three ways prayer can bring you closer to God.

3. How can prayer be a dialogue with God rather than a monologue?

4. Read each of the following verses aloud: Psalm 9:1-2; Matthew 7:7; Mark 9:7; 1 Thessalonians 5:18 and 1 John 1:9. What element of prayer do you find in each verse?

5. Have each person in the family demonstrate one of the elements of prayer by:

- Writing a definition of your element of prayer
- Explaining why your element of prayer is important
- Praying a prayer that reflects your particular element

6. Are all these elements of prayer necessary for a well-rounded life of prayer? Why or why not?

Reflect and Apply

1. The following is a list of potential prayer blockers. Read the list aloud, and then let each family member identify the items that cause the most problems for him or her in his or her prayer life.

   - Bad attitude
   - Not making prayer a priority
   - Falling asleep while praying
   - Hectic schedule
   - Don't feel God's presence
   - Guilt
   - Lack of faith that God is listening
   - Doubting His existence
   - Selfishness
   - Frustration in prayer
   - Daydreaming

2. Once each family member has identified one or more prayer blockers that most affect him or her, brainstorm together how he or she can overcome that problem. (Example: Hectic schedule—Pray every morning at 7:00 A.M., talk less on the phone.)

3. Now ask each person to identify which of the five elements he or she wants to put special emphasis on in his or her prayer life. Why?

4. Prayer is best learned by practice. As a family, take a few moments to pray together. Try to incorporate all of the five elements of prayer.

Note

1. "Woman Says Prayer Helped Her Win Lottery," *Headline News Discussion Starters* (Loveland, CO: Group, 1990), p. 31. Used by permission.

The Prayer of Relinquishment

Key Verse
I have been crucified with Christ and I no longer live,
but Christ lives in me. The life I live in the body, I live by faith
in the Son of God, who loved me and gave himself for me.
GALATIANS 2:20

The Big Idea
The prayer of relinquishment is a prayer of absolute surrender of your
will to God's will. The result is freedom and spiritual growth.

Focus

Read the following story aloud, and then use the questions to start a faith conversation.

> Far too often Christians act like the person in this story: "I would like to buy $3.00 worth of God, please. Not enough to explode my soul or disturb my sleep, but just enough to equal a cup of warm milk or a snooze in the sunshine. . . . I want ecstasy, not transformation; I want the warmth of the womb not a new birth. I want a pound of the Eternal in a paper sack. I would like to buy $3 worth of God, please."[1]

1. What do you think of this story?

2. What do you think is the difference between wanting only a little bit of God and wanting to live completely for God?

3. List three areas of your life in which you need to be more surrendered to God.

In the Word

Now discuss the following questions and get into the Word together:

1. The following is an inductive Bible study on one of the great secrets
   of the faith. With an "inductive study," you approach the Bible like
   a journalist, asking "who?" "what?" "where?" "when?" and "why?"
   Read Matthew 26:36-46 together.

   - **Who?** What persons are involved in this Scripture? Who
     wrote it?
   - **What?** What is taking place? How many times did Christ ask
     God to remove the cup? What was the "cup"? What is the
     prayer of relinquishment?
   - **Where?** Where is it happening?
   - **When?** When does this event take place during the life of Je-
     sus on earth?
   - **Why?** Why does Jesus pray the prayer of relinquishment? Are
     there consequences to this prayer? What are they?
   - **Well?** How does this prayer apply to your life?

2. Jesus said, "Father, if you are willing, take this cup from me; yet not
   my will, but yours be done" (Luke 22:42). Richard Foster calls the
   prayer of relinquishment a prayer of *self-emptying, surrender, abandon-
   ment, release* and *reservation*.[2] How do these words make sense in this
   episode of Jesus' life?

3. How can you apply these words to your own life?

4. What would be the results of a life of relinquishment?

5. Relinquishment is no easy task. Even Jesus struggled. It took three
   times to pray the same prayer, and He even had a bloody sweat last-
   ing long into the night. If you struggle with releasing your will to the
   Lord, then you are in good company. Read the following Scriptures
   together and discuss:

- Genesis 22:1-19: Abraham had to release his son Isaac.

- Exodus 7:1-6: Moses had to release his will for the sake of Israel and Egypt.

- 2 Samuel 12:16-22: David had to release his will for the son given by Bathsheba.

- 2 Corinthians 12:7-10: Paul had to release his desire to be free of his "thorn in the flesh."

Reflect and Apply

Perhaps Andrew Murray put it best: "The starting point and the goal of our Christian life is obedience." If there is a secret to living the Christian life, it is found through obedience. Through our obedient life come freedom and fulfillment.

1. Read John 14:21. If we say we love God, what will be the result according to this verse?

2. Why is this such an important principle in our Christian lives?

3. How does Galatians 2:20, "I have been crucified with Christ and I no longer live, but Christ lives in me. The life I live in the body, I live by faith in the Son of God, who loved me and gave himself for me," fit into the theme of a prayer of relinquishment?

4. Read Philippians 2:5-11. What attitude did Jesus have according to this Scripture? What was the result?

5. What can we do as a family to help one another live more obedient Christian lives?

Notes
1. Wilbur Rees, *$3.00 Worth of God* (Valley Forge, PA: Judson Press, 1971).
2. Richard J. Foster, *Prayer: Finding the Heart's True Home* (San Francisco, CA: Harper Collins, 1992), pp. 47-56.

Does God Answer Prayer?

Key Verse

But when you pray, go into your room, close the door and pray to your Father, who is unseen. Then your Father, who sees what is done in secret, will reward you.

MATTHEW 6:6

The Big Idea

God always answers prayer in one of three ways: no, go or grow.

Focus

Read the following story aloud, and then use the questions to start a faith conversation.

A 17-year-old girl died after a "faith healer" prayed for her healing and her parents pulled the plug on her life support machines. Against the wishes of the medical staff in the hospital, the parents of 17-year-old Debra Barker stopped her hospital respirator because they believed she was healed. Debra had been in a coma for three days after a tragic accident in which she was thrown from her car. Evidence showed the passengers of the car had been drinking.

Debra's pastor, Stephen Johnson, said that her parents asked Reverend Jesse Thomas, a faith healer who had just preached at their church, to come to the hospital to pray for their daughter. Reverend Thomas, Pastor Johnson and Debra's parents entered the hospital room at approximately 1:00 in the afternoon. After Reverend Thomas prayed for Debra, he said she was healed—he felt warmth flow through his hands onto her forehead. Debra's parents, "in faith," pulled the plug to the respirator without the permission of the hospital staff. Debra died 12 minutes later.

1. Was Reverend Thomas an evil man? Why or why not?

2. Did Debra's parents make a mistake?

3. Where does faith come into the healing process? Since the prayers were sincere, why didn't God heal Debra?

4. What lessons can we learn from this "news story"?

In the Word

When we ask God for something, He always answers our prayers. Sometimes we think the only time He answers prayer is when He says yes, but that is an improper view of prayer. Sometimes He says, "go." He says yes to our request and answers our prayer in the affirmative. Sometimes He says, "no." We ask in faith, but He knows best and it may be that what we asked for is not best for us. Other times God says, "grow." It might be a matter of timing and He wants us to wait on His will. With this in mind, discuss the following questions and get into the Word as a family:

1. When has God answered a prayer of yours with "go"? With "no"? With "grow"?

2. Read the following verses together and decide which of the three answers to prayer applies to the passage: Genesis 15:2-5, Luke 22:42, and Acts 3:1-10.

3. Read James 4:2-3. What does James 4:2 say to us today?

4. Read Matthew 6:5-8. What point(s) is Jesus making? What is the significance of this passage to your prayer life?

5. What makes an answer of "No" or "Grow" to our prayer so difficult to handle?

6. Why is "No" often a very good answer to prayer?

7. Where have you seen God's love and care in your life when He gave you an answer you weren't looking for?

Reflect and Apply

1. How do you feel knowing that God always answers prayer? Are you more or less likely to pray?

2. Below are statements about prayer. Read each statement aloud, and then have each family member indicate the degree to which he or she agrees with the statement (for example, "I strongly agree," "I strongly disagree," "I have no real opinion"). Remember that there are no right or wrong answers! Let each person self-evaluate without judgment from others.

   - I believe beyond a shadow of a doubt that God answers prayer.
   - I believe there is a God, but I question whether He is personally interested in everything I do.
   - I don't always know how God answers prayer, but I always have faith that He will.
   - When I don't see an obvious answer to my prayer, I begin to wonder if God answers at all.
   - I often thank God as well as ask for things.
   - I tend to treat God like Santa Claus—give me this; give me that.
   - When God says no, I feel it is for my own good.
   - When God says, "wait awhile," I can accept His timing without reservation.
   - When God answers my prayer, my faith is strengthened.
   - I often think my prayers being answered is just a coincidence.
   - I find myself praying throughout the day.
   - When I don't feel like praying is when I pray the hardest.
   - I don't pray in public.
   - I feel my prayer life is really growing.

3. Now take a few minutes to pray for each other. Specifically, ask God to grow each person's trust in Him.

The Lord's Prayer

Key Verses

This, then, is how you should pray: "Our Father in heaven, hallowed be your name, your kingdom come, your will be done on earth as it is in heaven. Give us today our daily bread. Forgive us our debts, as we also have forgiven our debtors. And lead us not into temptation, but deliver us from the evil one."

MATTHEW 6:9-13

The Big Idea

Jesus used the Lord's Prayer to teach His disciples how to pray. This powerful prayer is very relevant to our spiritual lives today.

Focus

Invite each family member to complete this sentence: "Prayer to me is more like _____ than _____."[1] Below are pairs of words or phrases—have each person choose between them to describe what prayer is like.

Prayer to me is more like _____ than _____.

a window	OR	a closet
listening	OR	talking
making a friend	OR	seeing an old friend
hard work	OR	a time of rest
a journey inward	OR	a journey outward
discipline	OR	fun

In the Word

The most famous prayer in the Scriptures is what Christians call the "Lord's Prayer." Jesus was teaching His disciples how to pray, using this prayer as an example. Many denominations repeat this prayer every week in their services. The beauty, intensity and significance of this prayer of Jesus are unequaled in Scripture. Read the Lord's Prayer in Matthew 6:9-13, and then answer the following questions together:

1. What is significant about the way Jesus addressed the Father?

2. How did Jesus place His life in the will of the Father?

3. What concerns does Jesus pray about in the prayer?

4. Read each line of the Lord's Prayer below, and then have each member of the family rewrite that line in his or her own words:

> Our Father in heaven
> hallowed be your name
> your kingdom come
> your will be done
> on earth as it is in heaven.
> Give us today our daily bread.
> Forgive us our debts
> as we also have forgiven our debtors
> and lead us not into temptation
> but deliver us from the evil one
> (Matthew 6:9-13).

5. According to the Lord's Prayer, why is our forgiveness from the Father conditional on our forgiving other people?

6. How might saying the Lord's Prayer become nothing more than an everyday ritual? What can we do to keep that from happening?

Reflect and Apply

1. What are some significant attitudes, requests and priorities found in the Lord's Prayer?

2. Do our family's priorities reflect the values Jesus emphasized in His prayer? Why or why not?

3. What are some specific ways we can honor God as a family?

4. What can we do to make God's will a bigger part of our lives?

5. How are we doing on forgiving each other? What can we do better?

6. How can we seek God's help in overcoming temptation?

Note
1. Adapted from *The Serendipity Bible Study Book* (Grand Rapids, MI: Zondervan, 1986), p. 33. Used by permission.

Developing a Disciplined Devotional Life

Key Verse

Very early in the morning, while it was still dark, Jesus got up, left the house and went off to a solitary place, where he prayed.

MARK 1:35

The Big Idea

Developing a disciplined devotional life is not an option, but a necessity for spiritual growth.

Focus

Imagine walking up to your mailbox and finding an envelope addressed to you. In the upper left-hand corner, where the return address is supposed to go, appears the word "God." Read the following letter aloud, and then use the questions to start a faith conversation:

My Dear Child,

I love you. I desire to spend as much time with you as possible. I took great joy in being part of your creation and your salvation. I consider My sacrifice for you a sign of My immeasurable love for you. My child, I want the best for you. I believe in you. I look forward to our daily times together. It gives Me great pleasure to spend time with you. Don't forget, I'm always with you.

Love, God

1. How would you feel?

2. What kind of decisions would you want to make about spending time with God?

3. The average person probably spends more than two hours a day watching television or surfing online, two hours a day listening to music, one hour a day dressing and grooming, and one hour a day eating. And yet the majority of people spend little or no time each day with God. A wise pastor once asked, "What is so important that you can't spend 15 minutes a day with God?" What's your answer?

4. What makes it so difficult to set up a regular daily time with God?

In the Word

Now discuss the following questions and get into the Word together.

1. First Timothy 4:7 states, "Train yourself to be godly." How do discipline and godliness walk hand in hand?

2. Mark 1:35 says, "Early in the morning, while it was still dark, Jesus got up, left the house and went off to a solitary place, where he prayed." According to Mark 1:29-34, Jesus experienced hectic days just like us! Why did He need to find a quiet place to be with God?

3. Joshua 1:8 states, "Do not let this Book of the Law depart from your mouth; meditate on it day and night, so that you may be careful to do everything written in it." What could this look like for our family?

4. First Peter 1:24-25 states, "For, 'All men are like grass, and all their glory is like the flowers of the field; the grass withers and the flowers fall, but the word of the Lord stands forever,' and this is the word that was preached to you." What does this tell us about the importance of the Word of God?

5. Proverbs 2:1-2,5 states, "My son, if you accept my words and store up my commands within you, turning your ear to wisdom and applying your heart to understanding, then you will understand the fear of the LORD and find the knowledge of God." Why is it important for us to be good listeners when we are trying to develop discipline?

Reflect and Apply

1. Now have a family time of reflection with God. Take the next 10 minutes to . . .

   • Read one or two or your favorite Scriptures.

   • Listen silently to the Lord during a time of prayer. Listen for the Holy Spirit to speak in a still, small voice or impression.

   • Practice the ACTS method of prayer (adoration, confession, thanksgiving and supplication). First, take two minutes to tell God of His greatness and His majestic power. *Adore* Him for who He is: the Lord of lords and the King of kings.

   • Take one minute to sit quietly before the Lord. Individually and silently, *confess* your sins to God. We keep the communication lines open when we confess our sins to God. Don't forget to thank Him for His forgiveness.

   • As a family, practice thank therapy by going around the group and *thanking* God for specific ways He has worked in your lives.

   • Now take two to five minutes and *ask* God for specific prayer requests. Pray for your family, church, school, friends, the government and yourself.

2. What are at least three ways a disciplined quiet time can bring you closer to God?

3. When is the best time of the day for you to take a few moments to be with the Lord?

4. How can you integrate creativity into your times with God?

5. What are some ways that we as a family can develop a stronger spiritual life together and also help each other with our individual time with God?

Worship

Key Verse
Come let us bow down in worship, let us kneel before the Lord our Maker.
PSALM 95:6

The Big Idea
Worship is an important but often misunderstood part of communication with God.

Focus

For each of the following words or phrases, have family members shout out the first thing that comes to mind. They shouldn't think too hard about the answer—just say whatever pops into their heads. When you've done that for each word, go back and discuss each family member's answer.

- Worship music
- Sermon
- Communion
- Offering
- Praying together
- Time with God

In the Word

Today, you will look at three important factors that go into worship: attitude, praise and prayers. Discuss the following questions and get into the Word together:

Attitude
1. Worship is honor and reverence paid to God. When we worship, we first give God our attitude. Read Psalm 122. What is the attitude of the person speaking in verse 1?

2. A great philosopher once said, "When it comes to worship we should never ask 'How was it?' We should ask 'How did I do?'" How is this statement different from what most people think of when it comes to worship?

3. To participate and enjoy a good worship experience, we need to develop a proper attitude toward worship. How do you prepare for your worship experience?

4. What specific things can you do to understand and enjoy your worship experience?

Praise

1. Next, we give God our praise. According to Psalm 122:3-4, why did the tribes of the Lord come to Jerusalem?

2. Read Psalm 100. How did you feel after you read the verses?

3. What relationship do you find between worship and praise?

4. Why should God receive our praise?

Prayers

1. Finally, we give God our prayers. Looking again at Psalm 122, what did the writer of this psalm pray for?

2. How is time spent with God in prayer a form of worship?

3. Reread verses 6-8 and remember that the setting is at least 2,500 years ago in Israel. How could you modernize these prayers and make them pertinent to your life today?

Reflect and Apply

1. Peace comes from a true worship of God. The dominant word in the last half of Psalm 122 is "peace." What do you think Jesus meant when He said, "Peace I leave with you; my peace I give you. I do not give to you as the world gives. Do not let your hearts be troubled and do not be afraid" (John 14:27)?

2. Why do you think peace could be a direct result of worship?

3. How does the worship of God affect how you feel about your problems and challenges?

4. What makes a worship experience boring or meaningless?

5. What activities do you like best in a worship service? In our times of family worship? In your personal worship time?

6. The next time you worship, how will you give God your attitude, your praise and your prayers?

Wrap up your family time with worship. Put on some music and sing along, then spend some time in prayer. If you came up with some good ideas for incorporating creativity in worship, try those out too!

The Bible

Key Verse

Do not let this Book of the Law depart from your mouth; meditate on it day and night, so that you may be careful to do everything written in it. Then you will be prosperous and successful.

JOSHUA 1:8

The Big Idea

The Bible plays an important role in our relationships with God. Studying God's Word is essential for spiritual growth.

Focus

You may have to go online to find the answers to the questions below. Have a race to see who can Google faster!

1. How many books are in the Bible?

2. How many books are in the Old Testament?

3. How many books are in the New Testament?

4. What language was the New Testament written in?

5. What language was the Old Testament mostly written in?

6. The New Testament is divided into four parts. Name the four parts.

7. The Old Testament is divided into four parts. Name the four parts.

8. Although most of the Old Testament was written in Hebrew and the New Testament in Greek, what was the language Jesus most often spoke?

In the Word

Now discuss the following questions and get into the Word together:

1. According to Joshua 1:8 and Psalm 1, what are the benefits of meditating on (thinking about) God's Word?

2. For a better understanding of why we should read the Bible, take a look at 2 Timothy 3:16-17. What does it say about Scripture?

3. Why is Scripture useful?

4. Some people have estimated that there are more than 3,000 promises in the Bible. Listed below are a number of biblical promises. Read the verses together, and then discuss how each promise might affect your lives as a family.

- Isaiah 26:3
- Isaiah 40:31
- Jeremiah 33:3
- Matthew 6:33

- John 14:14
- Philippians 4:6-7
- Philippians 4:19
- 1 John 5:14-15

Reflect and Apply

1. Why do you think God has given us the Bible?

2. What keeps you from spending more time in God's Word?

3. Together, brainstorm some of the possible results of not knowing or living out the following biblical principles:

- Galatians 5:14: "Love your neighbor as yourself." (Example: Treating other people disrespectfully.)
- Exodus 20:12: "Honor your father and your mother."
- 1 Thessalonians 4:3: "Avoid sexual immorality."

Below are two different daily Scripture reading plans. Look at these two plans together and invite each family member to choose one. When everyone has decided which plan he or she will follow, discuss the practicalities: Where is a good place to do your reading? What is a good time of day? The goal here is for each person to plan ahead to make God's Word a part of his or her daily life.

1. A Month of Praise and Wisdom
By reading less than 10 minutes a day for one month, you can go through the books of Psalms and Proverbs. The psalms are the beautiful songs of the Hebrew people, while the proverbs contain great, practical advice on many aspects of life. All you need to do is read five psalms and one proverb each day and after a month you will have completed two of the greatest books in the Bible. Then you will be ready for a new plan and you will already have started the positive habit of reading the Bible each day.

2. The 90-Day Experience[1]
Try an experiment that will change your life! You can read the entire New Testament in less than three months if you read approximately three chapters a day for 90 days. Listed is a format you can use to try this experiment. You'll be excited to see the positive results of incorporating biblical principles into your life.

1. Matthew 1–4
2. Matthew 5–7
3. Matthew 8–10
4. Matthew 11–13
5. Matthew 14–16
6. Matthew 17–19
7. Matthew 20–22
8. Matthew 23–25
9. Matthew 26–28
10. Mark 1–3
11. Mark 4–6
12. Mark 7–9
13. Mark 10–12
14. Mark 13–16
15. Luke 1–3
16. Luke 4–6
17. Luke 7–9
18. Luke 10–12

19. Luke 13–15
20. Luke 16–18
21. Luke 19–21
22. Luke 22–24
23. John 1–3
24. John 4–6
25. John 7–9
26. John 10–12
27. John 13–16:4
28. John 16:5–18
29. John 19–21
30. Acts 1–3
31. Acts 4–6
32. Acts 7–9
33. Acts 10–12
34. Acts 13–15
35. Acts 16–18
36. Acts 19–21:36
37. Acts 21:37–25:22
38. Acts 25:23–28:30
39. Romans 1–3
40. Romans 4–6
41. Romans 7–8
42. Romans 9–11

43. Romans 12–13
44. Romans 14–16
45. 1 Corinthians 1–4
46. 1 Corinthians 5–7
47. 1 Corinthians 8–11
48. 1 Corinthians 12–14
49. 1 Corinthians 15–16
50. 2 Corinthians 1–3
51. 2 Corinthians 4–6
52. 2 Corinthians 7–9
53. 2 Corinthians 1–13
54. Galatians 1–2
55. Galatians 3–4
56. Galatians 5–6
57. Ephesians 1–3
58. Ephesians 4–6
59. Philippians 1–2
60. Philippians 3–4
61. Colossians 1–2
62. Colossians 3–4
63. 1 Thessalonians 1–3
64. 1 Thessalonians 4–5
65. 2 Thessalonians 1–3
66. 1 Timothy 1–3

67. 1 Timothy 4–6
68. 2 Timothy 1–4
69. Titus 1–3
70. Philemon
71. Hebrews 1–2
72. Hebrews 3–4:13
73. Hebrews 4:14–7
74. Hebrews 8–10
75. Hebrews 11–13
76. James 1–3:12
77. James 3:13–5
78. 1 Peter 1–3:7
79. 1 Peter 3:8–5
80. 2 Peter 1–3
81. 1 John 1–3:10
82. 1 John 3:11–5
83. 2 John; 3 John; Jude
84. Revelation 1–3
85. Revelation 4–6
86. Revelation 7–9
87. Revelation 10–12
88. Revelation 13–15
89. Revelation 16–18
90. Revelation 19–22

Note
1. Jim Burns, *90 Days Through the New Testament* (Ventura, CA: Regal, 1990), pp. 15-135.

8

Getting Your Spiritual Life in Shape

Key Verse

Have nothing to do with godless myths and old wives' tales;
rather, train yourself to be godly.

1 TIMOTHY 4:7

The Big Idea

Although our salvation is a free gift, there are scriptural
principles that lead to spiritual growth and to getting
our spiritual lives in shape.

Focus

Goals are important. After all, if we don't have goals, how will we ever know if we've accomplished what we want to be and do in life?

1. Begin today's challenge by reading aloud each of the following statements. After each statement, have family members answer whether it is true or not in their lives.

   - I set goals for myself, but I seldom if ever reach them.

   - I set goals for myself, and I almost always reach them.

   - My goals in life are unclear. I am not really sure what I want to do.

   - My goals in life are well defined. They are a priority for me, and I work hard to achieve them.

- I know that goals are important, but I have a hard time figuring out what they should be or what steps I need to take to reach them.
- I've never set a goal in my life.

2. Here is an important exercise in goal setting. Have each person get a piece of paper and write out a short-term goal and a long-term goal for each area listed below. Note that short-term goals should be something that can be accomplished in one year, while long-term goals should take five to seven years to complete. Then, most importantly, have members describe what they will do to act on those goals.

- spiritual goals
- relationship goals (family and friends)
- school or career goals

3. Have the family members share their goals. Which goals in each section can they begin working on today?

In the Word

Now discuss the following questions and get into the Word together as a family:

1. Read Ephesians 6:10-18. After you have finished reading, go around the room and have each family member name one piece of equipment listed in the passage. For your reference, these are as follows:

- Belt of truth (verse 14)
- Breastplate of righteousness (verse 14)
- Shoes of the gospel of peace (verse 15)
- Shield of faith (verse 16)
- Helmet of salvation (verse 17)
- Sword of the Spirit (verse 17)

2. How is each piece of armor used in a spiritual battle?

3. Read 1 Corinthians 9:24-27. In a way, this passage represents Paul's philosophy of life. Although he uses imagery of runners in a race, he is really describing a battle. What type of battle is he describing?

4. What battles are you facing?

5. What would it take to win those battles?

6. What does Paul say that we need to do if we want to win the battle?

7. Would you consider yourself a disciplined person most of the time? Some of the time? Seldom, if ever? Why?

8. What common elements are there in the discipline of an athlete and spiritual discipline?

9. What will it take to become a more spiritually disciplined person?

10. We all need to know our goal. What was Paul's goal?

Conclude by having each person write one thing he or she can do this week to get his or her spiritual life in shape. Remind them that we are all running the race. It's a marathon, so we have to just keep at it!

Reflect and Apply

1. What keeps people from developing spiritual discipline in their lives?

2. What does this phrase mean: "He or she who aims at nothing gets there every time"?

3. Who do you know who has his or her spiritual life in shape? What steps did he or she take to get in shape?

4. What characteristics do you see in his or her life?

5. How much of your time and attention does God want?

6. Does God have your time and attention in every area of your life? Why or why not?

7. What can you do as a family to help each other improve and give every area of your lives over to God?

9

Praise

Key Verse
Let everything that has breath praise the Lord.
PSALM 150:6

The Big Idea
Praise is the purest form of worship. Praise frees our spirits to live for God.

Focus

Use the following questions to start a faith conversation:

1. What is praise?
2. How do we use it in our everyday lives? (For example, praising a dog for something well done.)
3. How do we use it with God?
4. Why do you think God deserves our praise?

Praise is the purest form of worship. When we begin to have an attitude of praise, we free our spirits to live for God. There is nothing more exciting than the experience of lifting up our hearts to God in praise. As a family, brainstorm some reasons to offer God your praise.

In the Word

Now get into the Word together. The following is a verse-by-verse study of Psalm 150 that will help you think about praise in the Bible and about how to apply it to your particular situation:

1. Read Psalm 150:1. Where do we praise God? Does our church find times every week to praise Him? How? What strength will we find when we learn to praise the Lord?

2. Read Psalm 150:2. What are "acts of power"? If God already knows how great He is, why do we need to tell Him?

3. Read Psalm 150:3-5. When the psalm was written, these were instruments commonly used to praise God. How do music and song relate to praise?

4. Read Psalm 150:6. Why should everything that breathes praise the Lord? How can we apply this verse to our daily lives?

5. Now read Psalm 34:1-10. According to this psalm, how often should we praise the Lord?

Reflect and Apply

1. Together, come up with a list of at least three spiritual principles you find in Psalms 34:1-10 and 150. Decide how each of you could apply these principles to your lives in the coming week.

2. Why is it important to have a consistent attitude of praise to God in our hearts?

3. How can praising God positively affect the other areas of our spiritual lives (thanksgiving, confession, servanthood, and so forth)?

4. If Jesus were physically sitting next to us right now, what would He say to us about how we praise Him?

5. Praise can lift our hearts up to the very throne of God. What are some difficulties that keep each of us from that special and holy place of God?

6. Have each family member share a reason they are filled with praise to the Lord. Then take a few moments to praise God for the reasons that were shared. You may want to go around in a circle and say, "Lord, I praise You because . . ."

10

Confession and Forgiveness

Key Verse

*If we confess our sins, he is faithful and just and will forgive us our sins
and purify us from all unrighteousness.*

1 JOHN 1:9

The Big Idea

*The spiritual act of confession is an essential element in our prayer lives.
The natural result of confession is forgiveness in Christ.*

FOCUS

Max Lucado is my favorite Christian author. He tells a story that I will
never forget of a mother and her four-year-old daughter. Read the following story, and then use the questions to start a faith conversation.

> Susanna (the mom) and her daughter, Gayaney, were trying on
> clothes at her sister-in-law's home when the worst earthquake in
> the history of Armenia hit. There were 55,000 victims in this
> one quake.
>
> One minute they were on the fifth floor of an apartment
> building; the next they knew they had tumbled into the base-
> ment. Susanna and Gayaney were still alive, but they were stuck
> and could not get up. "Mommy, I need a drink," said the little
> girl. "Please give me something," Susanna found a 24-ounce jar of
> blackberry jam that had fallen into the basement. She gave the
> entire jar to her daughter to eat. It was gone by the second day.
>
> "Mommy, I'm thirsty." Susanna didn't know what to do.
> Truthfully, there was nothing she could do to help her daughter.
> They were cold and numb, and she lost hope. Periodically Su-
> sanna would sleep, but usually she awakened from the whining
> and whimpering of her precious daughter.

"Mommy, I'm thirsty. Please give me something to drink." Then Susanna remembered that it was possible to drink blood! So she cut her left index finger and gave it to her daughter to suck. The drops of blood were not enough. "Please, Mommy, some more. Cut another finger." Susanna had no idea how many times she cut herself, but if she hadn't Gayaney would have died. Susanna's blood was her daughter's only hope.[1]

Max Lucado writes about this episode this way: "Beneath the rubble of a fallen world, [Jesus] pierced his hands. In the wreckage of a collapsed humanity he ripped open his side. His children were trapped, so he gave freely his own blood. It was all he had. His friends were gone. His strength was waning, his possessions had been gambled away at his feet. Even his father turned his head. His blood was all he had. But his blood was all it took. If anyone is thirsty, Jesus once said, let him come to me and drink. And the hand was pierced. And the blood was poured. And the children were saved."[2]

1. Read Hebrews 9:11-22. What is the significance of blood and forgiveness?

2. Why is the blood of Christ different from the blood of goats?

3. What does verse 22 mean?

In the Word

Now discuss the following questions and get into the Word together:

1. Read John 8:1-11. If you were the woman, how would you feel?

2. What do you think happened to the man who was caught with the woman but not brought to Jesus?

3. What points are important to remember from the conversation with Jesus and the woman in John 8:9-11?

4. The word "confess" actually means *to agree*. Confessing our sins to God is agreeing with God that we, like everyone else, fall short of perfection.

Read these verses on confession and forgiveness together, and then discuss what they mean.

- 1 John 1:9
- Psalm 86:5
- Isaiah 1:18
- Hebrews 10:17

5. Jeremiah 31:34 states, "For I will forgive their wickedness and will remember their sins no more." According to this verse, what will Christ do with our confessed sins?

6. Why is it sometimes easier to accept God's forgiveness than to forgive ourselves?

7. Read James 5:16. What makes confession to another person such a powerful experience?

8. Where does the idea of repentance come into the picture of forgiveness?

Reflect and Apply

Saint Peter's Square, May 1981, was the scene of a terrible event that shocked the world: an assassination attempt on Pope John Paul II. The scene was quite different nearly three years later when Pope John Paul sat in Rome's Rebibbia Prison holding the hand of his would-be assassin, Mehment Ali Agca. The Pope forgave the man for the shooting. What a tremendous story of forgiveness and reconciliation. While the Pope whispered quietly in the cell, he preached a message loud and clear to the entire world. He communicated the message of Christ.

1. How would you feel about a man who attempted to kill you?

2. What do you think the assassin was feeling after the Pope's message of forgiveness?

3. How can you proclaim the same message of Christ in your world and family today?

4. Unfortunately, it is uncommon in our world to forgive and forget. Most people do not cancel debts, especially large ones. But Jesus does. Why is confession and repentance an important process of our faith in Christ?

5. Read Matthew 6:14-15. How does God's forgiveness for you affect the way you treat others?

6. Do you need to cancel a debt by extending forgiveness to someone who has wronged you, whether he or she is in the family or outside the family?

Notes
1. Jim Burns, *Spirit Wings* (Ann Arbor, MI: Vine Books, 1992), pp. 188-189.
2. Max Lucado, *The Applause of Heaven* (Dallas, TX: Word, Inc., 1990), p. 91.

11

Thanksgiving

Key Verse

Give thanks in all circumstances, for this is God's will for you in Christ Jesus.

1 THESSALONIANS 5:18

The Big Idea

Creating an attitude of thankfulness is definitely a life-changing experience.
Thankful people are happy people.

Focus

The following is known as "The Serenity Prayer," written by Friedrich Christoph Oetinger. Read this prayer aloud, and then use the questions to start a faith conversation.

Lord, give me the serenity
To accept the things I cannot change;
Give me the courage
To change the things I can, and
The wisdom to distinguish
The one from the other.

1. What truths do you find in this prayer?

2. How can we, as a family, use this prayer to make our family stronger?

3. For what do you need serenity? For what do you need courage?

4. How can prayer keep you focused on giving thanks to God?

Pray for the situations just discussed. Then list how as family members you can help and encourage each other in the situations.

In the Word

Christians have much to be thankful for, yet we all struggle at times with being ungrateful servants in our Father's house. There are two points that can help us to be more thankful people: (1) having the right attitude, and (2) making it a habit in our lives. Keeping these two aspects in mind, discuss the following questions and get into the Word together.

Thankfulness Is an Attitude

1. Read 1 Thessalonians 5:18, and then have members finish the following sentence: "When I read that I should be thankful in all situations, I . . ."

2. Does this Scripture say to be thankful *for* all situations?

3. It would be ridiculous to be thankful for a negative problem. However, how would making an effort to be thankful in all circumstances help you to better see that even in difficult times, there are reasons to be grateful to God?

4. What's a difficult situation that you are experiencing right now? What's one thing that you can be thankful for in that situation?

Make Thankfulness a Habit in Your Life

1. Read Romans 5:8. What is the good news found in this verse?

2. How can this point help you be thankful even when things are getting difficult?

3. Why do we tend to focus on the negative instead of the positive?

4. What are several reasons why thankful people are usually happier people?

5. Why do you think Christmas and Easter are special times of thanksgiving for Christians?

6. How do you think it makes God feel when we are thankful?

7. How do you think it makes God feel when we complain?

"Thank therapy" can help us put into practice Paul's command to "be thankful in all situations." Thank therapy is writing on paper 20 reasons why you are thankful. At first glance, 20 reasons may look like a lot, but as you begin writing, you'll find that you can easily list 20 reasons. You'll see how helpful it is to be reminded of God's blessings in your life. As you become consciously aware of why you are thankful to God for what He has already done for you, great things will begin to develop in your spirit. Give it a try! When you are done, share a few with your family.

Reflect and Apply

1. How can we practice thankfulness in our home more often?

2. What is the significance of these quotes? Read and discuss them.

   - "I complained because I had no shoes until I met a man who had no feet."

   - "Thankfulness transcends your circumstances. Your circumstances may never change, but your attitude can change and that makes all the difference in the world."

3. How will you take the principles of thankfulness and use them in your life this week?

As you wrap up your family time, play the Thankfulness Bombardment Game. Each family member completes this sentence for every other family member: "I am thankful to God for [family member's name] because . . ."

12

Asking

Key Verse

So I say to you: Ask and it will be given to you; seek and you will find; knock and the door will be opened to you. For everyone who asks receives; he who seeks finds; and to him who knocks, the door will be opened.

LUKE 11:9

The Big Idea

God is a loving Lord who hears the persistent prayers of His children.

Focus

Use the following questions to start a faith conversation:

1. What comes to your mind when you think about prayer?
2. What is the absolutely best place for you to pray? Why?
3. What is the worst place for you to pray? Why?
4. What is the hardest thing about prayer? Why?
5. What is the greatest thing about prayer? Why?

In the Word

Read Luke 11:5-10, and then answer the following questions as a family:

1. What characteristics of the friend at the door caused the person to finally open up the door?

2. What was the point of Jesus' story?

3. What kind of invitation do we receive in Luke 11:9-10?

4. What do you think keeps most believers from asking, seeking and knocking more often?

5. It is important to note that the Greek words translated into English as *ask, knock* and *seek* are all written in the present tense, which is best translated: keep on asking, keep on knocking and keep on seeking. How does this knowledge help your understanding of verses 9 and 10?

6. Now read Luke 11:11-13. Why do you think Jesus compared the gifts of a good earthly father with the response of our heavenly Father?

7. Now read Matthew 21:22, Hebrews 11:1 and 1 John 5:14-15. How do these verses influence your attitude about prayer?

8. What are you asking God to accomplish in your life?

Reflect and Apply

1. What is the greatest need you have and want to give to God in prayer?

2. Now spend some quality time together with God in prayer. The following is a list of needs you might include:

   - Pray for the needs of our community, school, job.
   - Pray for the needs of our church.
   - Pray for the needs of missions, the "10/40 Window" (the people in the area of the world from 10 degrees to 40 degrees north latitude).
   - Pray for our president and government leadership.

- Pray for the personal purity and lifestyle of our church leaders. (Don't forget to thank God for them.)
- Pray for your family (specifically and by name).
- Pray for your own life.
- Listen to the names the Spirit places on your mind and pray for them.

Conclude by creating a prayer request list for your family. Start with the individual needs that each family member gave and ask for others to volunteer to pray specifically for that need in the coming week. During next week's family time, get updates from everyone regarding answered prayer, and then update the list. In just a few weeks, you'll have a record of God's work in your family's life!

13

God's Unconditional Love

Key Verse

But we had to celebrate and be glad, because this brother of yours was dead and is alive again; he was lost and is found.

LUKE 15:32

The Big Idea

God loves you unconditionally, not for what you do but for who you are: His child.

Focus

Read the following story aloud, and then use the questions to start a faith conversation:

> Once upon a time there was a young girl named Susie. She was a beautiful little girl with the most wonderful doll collection in the world. Her father traveled all over the world on business, and for nearly 12 years he had brought dolls home to Susie. In her bedroom, she had shelves of dolls from all over the United States and from every continent on Earth. She had dolls that could sing and dance and do just about anything a doll could possibly do.
>
> One day, one of her father's business acquaintances came to visit. At dinner he asked Susie about her wonderful doll collection. After dinner Susie took him by the hand and showed him these marvelous dolls from all over the world. He was very impressed. After he took the grand tour and was introduced to many of the beautiful dolls, he asked Susie, "With all these precious dolls, you must have one that is

your favorite. Which one is it?" Without a moment's hesitation Susie went over to her old beat-up toy box and started pulling out toys. From the bottom of the box she pulled out one of the most ragged dolls you have ever seen. There were only a few strands of hair left on the head. The clothing had long since disappeared. The doll was filthy from many years of play outside. One of the buttons for the eyes was hanging down with only one strand of string to keep it connected. Stuffing was coming out at the elbow and knee. Susie handed the doll to the gentleman and said, "This doll is my favorite."

The man was shocked and asked, "Why this doll with all these beautiful dolls in your room?"

She replied, "If I didn't love this doll nobody would!"

That single statement moved the businessman to tears. It was such a simple statement, yet so profound. The little girl loved her doll unconditionally. She loved the doll not for its beauty or abilities but simply because it was her very own.

1. How does this story relate to the love God has for us?

2. Are there any stories in the Bible that remind you of this story?

3. Why do many people have a hard time accepting God's unconditional love?

In the Word

Read Luke 15:11-32. Notice that this story has three main characters: (1) the younger (prodigal) son, (2) the father, and (3) the older (faithful) son. Keeping these characters in mind, answer the following questions together:

The Younger Son

1. What did the younger son request from his father?

2. What did the son do after he received his request?

3. In the far country, this Jewish son worked on a pig farm (see verses 15-16). The Jews who follow Old Testament Law do not eat pork; pigs are listed in the Law as an unclean animal. Knowing this, what is the significance of the son's occupation?

4. What was the result of the son's choices and actions?

The Father

1. How did the father respond to the son's coming home? Was this the expected response?

2. According to Luke 15:7-10, how does God respond to the homecoming of a lost sinner?

The Older Son

1. Why do you think the older brother reacted the way he did?

2. What was the father's response to the older brother?

Reflect and Apply

1. How does verse 32 summarize the entire parable?

2. Ask each family member to identify the character (younger son, father or older son) that best describes how he or she feels about his or her relationship with God, and explain why.

3. How does it feel knowing that your heavenly Father, like the father in this story, has paid the price for your sin and celebrates when His children return to Him?

4. Read Romans 5:8. How does this verse relate to this story?

5. Why is it often difficult to receive unconditional love from God or even others?

6. What makes the concept of God's loving us unconditionally so inviting?

7. How would you describe God's love to someone who had never heard about it before?

Be sure to stress to your family that no matter what we do or don't do, God loves us! The love we receive from family or friends can change, but God's love for us always remains the same because God doesn't change. While we may know this, we may not always experience it. Pray together that God will make His love for each of you known to your minds and experienced by your hearts.

14

New Life

Key Verse

For God so loved the world that he gave his one and only Son,
that whoever believes in him shall not perish but have eternal life.

JOHN 3:16

The Big Idea

Because Jesus Christ died for our sins, we can have a brand-new
life and relationship with God.

Focus

Read the following story aloud, and then use the questions to start a faith conversation:

Once upon a time, there lived a group of people called the Laconians. The Laconians lived in a rural setting; a forest surrounded their village. They looked and acted a lot like you and I do. They dressed like we dress and went to school and worked like we work. They even had the same family struggles and search for identity that we have. But there was one major difference. Connected to the ankle of every Laconian was a brace, and attached to the brace was a strong metal chain, and connected to the chain was a round, heavy metal ball.

Wherever the Laconians went or whatever they did, they carried the ball and chain. Yet no one seemed to mind. After all, they were used to the ball and chain, and no one in Laconia was free from the bondage of the ball and chain.

One day the hero of the story, Tommy, was exploring in the forest after school when he went around a corner, slipped and fell . . . and the chain broke. Tommy had never heard of a chain breaking before in the land of Laconia, and he was terrified. But he was also curious. As he stood and stared at the broken chain, he sensed that something very significant had happened in his life. In fact, he tried to take a step without the ball and chain and almost fell down. After all, he wasn't used to the freedom of walking without this bondage.

Tommy quickly slipped the ball and chain back on his ankle. He told no one of his new discovery. The next day after school this new curiosity drove him back to the forest to experiment with his newfound freedom. This time when he unhooked the chain he walked. Yes, it was wobbly, but he quickly learned to compensate, and in a few hours he was running and jumping and even trying to climb the trees in the forest. Every day after school he found himself out in the forest, free to experience life in a different way from anyone else in Laconia.

He decided to share his secret with his best friend. After school one day he brought his friend to the forest and showed him his new freedom. But his friend responded by saying, "Don't be different! Once a Laconian, you'll always be a Laconian. Be happy with what you have." This response only put more fuel in Tommy's fire. He knew he needed to show all the people of his little village that they could be set free.

One spring day when the whole village was outside, Tommy took the ball and placed it under his arm, then ran and skipped through the town. He wanted to show the people of his village his joy and freedom. Their response was that of shock. They mocked him, scolded him and challenged him to not be different. Even his family told him to immediately become a normal part of the community and put his chain back on.

Tommy knew then and there that since he had experienced this freedom he could never again settle for second best in his life. For Tommy, mediocrity was out of the question. He would choose to be different . . . and he was different from then on.

This story is for people who don't want to settle for second best in life. Jesus said, "You will know the truth and the truth will set you free" (John 8:32). You don't have to live a life of boring mediocrity. God's desire for your life is to break the chain that holds you back and to give your life to His purpose. You can choose to be different.

1. Read John 10:10. How could understanding this promise be like making a new discovery?

2. What is keeping you from breaking the chain and living the life of freedom God wants for you?

In the Word

Read John 3:1-21. Before you begin to discuss this passage, you might want to provide some background information. For the most part, Jesus was surrounded by the ordinary people of His day. However, in this conversation, we see Him with one of the important Jewish leaders of His time. Nicodemus was a Pharisee, and in some ways the Pharisees were the most important people in the whole country of Israel. There were never more than 6,000 at a time, and they all were completely dedicated to observing every detail of the Old Testament Law. Nicodemus was also a member of the Sanhedrin, which was composed of 70 religious leaders. The Sanhedrin was the supreme court of the Jewish people. Now answer the following questions as a family:

1. What is the significance of an important man like Nicodemus talking with Jesus about being born again?

2. Why do you suppose Nicodemus came to Jesus at night?

3. What is the main theme of this conversation?

4. This conversation between Jesus and Nicodemus is sometimes confusing to people. What questions do you have about what Jesus said?

5. If Jesus came to you and declared, "I tell you the truth, no one can see the kingdom of God unless he is born again" (John 3:3), how would you respond?

6. To be "born again" literally means to be born spiritually from above. What great message of hope do you see in this passage?

7. How does John 3:16 validate the idea that new life begins with God's love?

8. How does this passage give you the assurance of your salvation in Christ (see verses 8,16)?

Reflect and Apply

1. What does "new life in Christ" mean to you?

2. What holds people back from starting over with God?

3. What steps of faith do you need to take right now?

15

A Lifestyle of Love

Key Verses

*The woman said, "I know that Messiah" (called Christ) "is coming.
When he comes, he will explain everything to us."
Then Jesus declared, "I who speak to you am he."*

JOHN 4:25-26

The Big Idea

*Our lives and actions are our greatest witness. You must earn the right
to be heard, and then speak the truths of Jesus Christ.*

Focus

Read the story below, and then answer the following questions to start
a faith conversation:

> I saw a strange sight. I stumbled upon a story most strange,
> like nothing my life, my street sense, my sly tongue had ever
> prepared me for.
>
> Hush, child. Hush, now, and I will tell it to you.
>
> Even before the dawn one Friday morning I noticed a
> young man, handsome and strong, walking on the alleys of our
> City. He was pulling an old cart filled with clothes both bright
> and new, and he was calling in a clear, tenor voice: "Rags!"
>
> "Now, this is a wonder," I thought to myself, for the man
> stood six-feet-four, and his arms were like tree limbs, hard
> and muscular, and his eyes flashing intelligence. Could he
> find no better job than this, to be a ragman in the inner city?
>
> I followed him. My curiosity drove me. And I wasn't dis-
> appointed.

Soon the Ragman saw a woman sitting on her back porch. She was sobbing into a handkerchief, sighing, and shedding a thousand tears. Her knees and elbows made a sad X. Her shoulders shook. Her heart was breaking.

The Ragman stopped his cart. Quietly, he walked to the woman, stepping round tin cans, dead toys and Pampers.

"Give me your rag," he said so gently, "and I'll give you another."

He slipped the handkerchief from her eyes. She looked up, and he laid across her palm a linen cloth so clean and new that it shined. She blinked from the gift to the giver.

Then, as he began to pull his cart again, the Ragman did a strange thing: he began to weep, to sob as grievously as she had done, his shoulders shaking. Yet she was left without a tear.

"This is a wonder," I breathed to myself, and followed the sobbing Ragman like a child who cannot turn away from mystery.

"Rags! Rags! New rags for old!"

In a little while, when the sky showed grey behind the rooftops and I could see the shredded curtains hanging out black windows, the Ragman came upon a girl whose head was wrapped in a bandage, whose eyes were empty. Blood soaked her bandage. A single line of blood ran down her cheek.

Now the tall Ragman looked upon this child with pity, and he drew a lovely yellow bonnet from his cart.

"Give me your rag," he said, tracing his own line of her cheek, "and I'll give you mine."

The child could only gaze at him while he loosened the bandage, removed it, and tied it to his own head. The bonnet he set on hers. And I gasped at what I saw for with the bandage went the wound! Against his brow ran a darker, more substantial blood—his own!

"Rags! Rags! I take old rags!" cried the sobbing, bleeding, strong, intelligent Ragman.

The sun hurt both the sky, now, and my eyes; the Ragman seemed more and more to hurry.

"Are you going to work?" he asked a man who leaned against a telephone pole. The man shook his head.

The ragman pressed him: "Do you have a job?"

"Are you crazy?" sneered the other. He pulled away from the pole, revealing the right sleeve of his jacket—flat, the cuff stuffed into the pocket. He had no arm.

"So," said the Ragman. "Give me your jacket, and I'll give you mine."

Such quiet authority in his voice!

The one-armed man took off his jacket. So did the Ragman—and I trembled at what I saw: For the Ragman's arm stayed in its sleeve, and when the other put it on he had two good arms, thick as tree limbs; but the Ragman had only one.

"Go to work," he said.

After that he found a drunk, lying unconscious beneath an army blanket, an old man, hunched, wizened, and sick. He took that blanket and wrapped it around himself, but for the drunk he left new clothes.

And now I had to run to keep up with the Ragman. Though he was weeping uncontrollably, and bleeding freely at the forehead, pulling his cart with one arm, stumbling from drunkenness, falling again and again, exhausted, old, old and sick, yet he went with terrible speed. On spider's legs he skittered through the alleys of the City, this mile and the next, until he came to its limits, and then he rushed beyond.

I wept to see the change in this man. I hurt to see his sorrow. And yet I needed to see where he was going in such haste, perhaps to know what drove him so.

The little Ragman—he came to a landfill. He came to the garbage pits. And then I wanted to help him in what he did, but I hung back, hiding. He climbed a hill. With tormented labor he cleared a little space on that hill. Then he sighed. He lay down. He pillowed his head on a handkerchief and a jacket. He covered his bones with an army blanket and he died.

Oh, how I cried to witness that death! I slumped in a junked car and wailed and mourned as one who has no hope—because I had come to love the Ragman. Every other face had faded in the wonder of this man, and I cherished him; but he died. I sobbed myself to sleep.

I did not know—how could I know?—that I slept through Friday night and Saturday and its night, too.

But then, on Sunday morning, I was awakened by violence.

Light—pure, hard, demanding light—slammed against my sour face, and I blinked, and I looked, and I saw the last and the first wonder of all. There was the Ragman, folding the blanket most carefully, a scar on his forehead, but alive! And, besides that, healthy! There was no sign of sorrow nor of age, and all the rags that he had gathered shined for cleanliness.

Well, then I lowered my head and trembling for all that I had seen, I myself walked up to the Ragman. I told him my name with shame, for I was a sorry figure next to him. Then I took off all my clothes in that place, and I said to him with a dear yearning in my voice: "Dress me."

He dressed me. My Lord, he put new rags on me, and I am a wonder beside him. The Ragman, the Ragman, the Christ![1]

1. What do you think of this story?

2. What makes the story of the Ragman so powerful?

3. How does the person of Jesus relate to the Ragman story?

In the Word

Read John 4:39-42 together, and then answer the following questions:

1. In this portion of the gospel, Jesus shares His faith and life with a Samaritan woman. It was almost unthinkable for a Jew to speak with a Samaritan and definitely unheard of for a Jewish rabbi to speak to a woman—much less a Samaritan woman. Yet we find Jesus not only speaking to her but also asking to share a drink of water and caring for her spiritual relationship with God. Why do you suppose the woman was so surprised that Jesus asked her for a drink of water (see verses 7-9)?

2. What do you think Jesus meant by "living water" (see verses 10-15)?

3. What do you suppose Jesus was trying to accomplish from the conversation in verses 16-26?

4. What makes the declaration of Jesus in verse 26 one of the key statements of all Scripture?

5. What are a couple of reasons why the Samaritans in the town of Sychar believed (see verses 39-42)?

6. Notice that Jesus did not condemn the woman. Why would condemning her not have helped His relationship with her?

7. What did Jesus do instead to lead the conversation?

8. In this conversation, the woman began to get sidetracked. How did Jesus lead her back to the central issue?

9. What are some ways we can let people know we care for them even when we disapprove of their lifestyle?

10. Jesus confronted the woman with the fact that He was the Messiah. Now she had to respond. What are some ways we can help our friends and family have a positive encounter with the person of Jesus Christ?

11. What are the results shown in John 4:39-42 of Jesus' conversation with the Samaritan woman?

Reflect and Apply

1. What is one of your first memories of hearing about God?

2. What people have been positive spiritual influences in your life?

3. When did God become real in your life? (If you aren't sure if He has, it's okay to share that.)

4. What attracted you to Christianity?

5. Why are some Christians afraid to share their faith?

6. What happens when witnessing turns into condemnation of non-Christians?

7. What questions can arouse curiosity about Christianity?

8. How can we put into practice the meaning of the Ragman story and share the love of God with those who aren't Christians?

Note

1. Walter Wanagerin, Jr., *Ragman and Other Cries of Faith* (San Francisco, CA: Harper and Row, 1984). Used by permission.

16

Discipleship

Key Verse
Then he called the crowd to him along with his disciples and said: "If anyone would come after me, he must deny himself and take up his cross and follow me."

MARK 8:34

The Big Idea
Discipleship is obediently denying yourself and following the Lord Jesus Christ.

Focus

Together, brainstorm activities or events that fit the following categories:

- Five activities for free
- Three activities for $1 to $20
- Three activities for $20 to $100
- Three activities for more than $100

Now do the same for the following:

- Five aspects of the Christian life that are free
- Three aspects of the Christian life that are costly, but not too costly
- Three costly aspects of the Christian life
- Three extremely costly aspects of the Christian life

In the Word

Read Mark 8:34-37 together. In this passage, Jesus gives three requirements to those who want to be His disciples: (1) they must deny themselves, (2) they must take up their cross, and (3) they must follow Him. Keeping these three requirements in mind, answer the following questions:

Deny Yourself

1. What does it mean to "deny yourself"?

2. We belong to Christ, not ourselves. We were bought for a high price. In order to follow Christ, we must sometimes deny our own needs for the sake of Christ's purposes. What does Paul say in Galatians 2:20 about denying yourself?

3. How does Galatians 2:20 apply to your life?

Take Up Your Cross

1. What does it mean to "take up your cross"?

2. Are you willing to accept the cost of becoming Christ's person in your home, school, love life and family relationships?

3. Brainstorm specific ways you can take up your cross in the above situations.

"Follow Me"

1. Following Jesus means to be willing to go anywhere and do anything for Him. Are you willing to follow Jesus wherever He leads you?

2. How are you being obedient to this part of the Scripture?

Reflect and Apply

1. What will it take for you to give more of your time and attention to passionately pursuing Christ? (This is the most important question of this chapter!)

2. What makes discipleship costly?

3. Why is it difficult to deny ourselves, take up our cross and follow Jesus?

4. What are the parts of your life that are holding you back from all that God has for you? What can you do to yield these parts of your life to God's purpose?

17

Setting a Strong Foundation

Key Verse

Therefore everyone who hears these words of mine and puts them into practice is like a wise man who built his house on the rock.

MATTHEW 7:24

The Big Idea

When you set a solid faith foundation, you will be able to withstand the trials of life.

Focus

Read the story below, and then answer the following questions to start a faith conversation:

In 1923, eight of the world's most successful financiers were living the good life. To all accounts it seemed as if they truly had "gained the whole world," and the future looked incredibly bright. But by 25 years later, each of the men had either filed bankruptcy, served time in prison or committed suicide.

Charles M. Schwab, president of the Bethlehem Steel Company, led an opulent lifestyle that included extravagant parties and high-stakes gambling sprees. Before the stock market crash of 1929, he spent between $25 to $40 million dollars, roughly equivalent to $275 to $440 million dollars in today's currency. He lived his final years on borrowed money and died $300,000 in debt.

Samuel Insull was a founding partner of what would become General Electric. At one point, his personal fortune was estimated between $73 million to $300 million. When his empire collapsed during the Great Depression, he was charged with mail fraud and antitrust charges and fled to Greece. He died at age 78 from a heart attack in Paris with 20 cents in his pocket.

Howard C. Hopson, president of Associated Gas and Electric Company, at one time had a fortune of $74 million. After the stock market crash of 1929, he was investigated by the Securities and Exchange Commission and filed bankruptcy. He was convicted of mail fraud and sentenced to five years in prison. He died in Brooklea Sanitarium in 1949.

Arthur William Cutten, the country's greatest wheat speculator, was one of the country's richest citizens in the 1920s. He lost more than $50 million in the stock market crash of 1929 and was ultimately charged with improper trading activities and income tax evasion. He died of a heart attack in 1936 before he could stand trial.

Richard Whitney was elected president of the New York Stock Exchange in 1929. He is reported to have spent up to $5,000 per month during the height of the Great Depression, and as he fell deeper into debt to maintain his lifestyle, he turned to embezzlement. In 1938 he was convicted and sentenced to a term of 5 to 10 years in Sing Sing prison (he served three years before receiving parole).

Albert B. Fall was a rancher, lawyer, prospector, miner, legislator and U.S. senator. He was appointed to Secretary of Interior by President Harding in 1921, but resigned in 1923 after being implicated in the Teapot Dome Scandal. He was convicted in 1929 of accepting a bribe from an oilman and was fined $100,000, which he stated he now was unable to pay. He was also sentenced to one year in prison.

Jesse Lauriston Livermore, known as the "Great Bear" and "Boy Plunger," was one of the most flamboyant and successful market speculators in the history of Wall Street. While most people lost money in the stock market crash of 1929, Livermore made an estimated $100 million. He lost this entire fortune by 1934 and declared bankruptcy. In 1940, he shot himself in a hotel room in New York.

Ivar Krueger was a Swedish businessman who founded a multi-billion-dollar match conglomerate. Like many of the others on this list, he was essentially running a huge pyramid scheme. When the company went under in early 1932—the largest bankruptcy of its time—investors lost millions of dollars. Kreuger shot himself in March of 1932.[1]

1. What was the basis of these men's lives?

2. What was missing in all of these men's lives? Why is it so easy to slide into the same kinds of goals as these men?

3. What does Matthew 6:21,24 mean for you today?

4. How do these verses relate to setting a firm spiritual foundation?

In the Word

Read Matthew 7:24-27. Notice that in each case, the rain came, the streams rose and the wind blew and beat against the house. Problems come to everyone regardless of spiritual maturity or lifestyle. The major difference is that when problems come, the person with a strong base will be able to withstand the attack. Christians are not free from problems. We must prepare for difficulties by developing a solid foundation. What's great is that we don't need to develop it on our own—God will help. Keeping this in mind, answer the following questions together as a family:

1. To build any structure, you must first lay a cornerstone. A cornerstone is a stone set at the bottom of a structure. Read 1 Peter 2:4-8. Who is clearly the Cornerstone in this Scripture?

2. Is this Cornerstone a part of your life? If not, what or who is?

3. It is important to follow the instructions to set a strong foundation properly. Read John 14:15,21. What do these verses tell us to do if we love God?

4. What is the result of obedience, according to verse 21?

5. How do Jesus' statements in these verses relate to Joshua 1:8 and Psalm 1:2-3?

6. Growth is slow, and it takes time. Setting a strong foundation is a lifelong process. Slow, consistent growth is a sure way to spiritual maturity. Read Philippians 3:12-14. How do these wise words of Paul deal with setting a strong foundation slowly?

7. Read Joshua 1:8 and Psalm 1:2-3. What is the result of spending time with God each day?

8. What example does Jesus give us in Mark 1:35?

Reflect and Apply

1. Read the following quote aloud: "Don't say you don't have enough time. You have exactly the same number of hours per day that were given to Helen Keller, Pasteur, Michelangelo, Mother Teresa, Leonardo da Vinci, Thomas Jefferson and Albert Einstein."[2] What does this mean to you as it relates to how you spend your time?

2. Many people argue that they are too busy to set aside time to spend with Jesus each day. In light of this, have your family members calculate the top five things on which they spend their time and how much time they spend on that each day. (For example: sleeping, watching TV, playing video games, working, talking on the phone or texting, playing sports.)

3. When do you set aside time with Jesus during your day? Or, if you don't already, where could you make time in the day to spend in prayer and study?

Notes

1. Jim Burns, *Uncommon Stories and Illustrations* (Ventura, CA: Gospel Light, 2008), pp. 148-149.

2. H. Jackson Brown, *Life's Little Instruction Book* (Nashville, TN: Rutledge Hill, 1991).

Obedience

Key Verse

Whoever has my commands and obeys them, he is the one who loves me.
He who loves me will be loved by my Father, and I too will love him
and show myself to him.

JOHN 14:21

The Big Idea

If there is a secret to the Christian life, it is found in obedience.

Focus

Read the following story, and then answer a few questions to start a faith conversation:

On August 17, 1859, Charles Blondin, arguably one of the best tightrope walkers of all time, stretched a tightrope across Niagara Falls. People came by train from Buffalo, New York and Toronto, Canada to see him walk across the tightrope that was suspended high above the raging falls.

The story is told that as Blondin stepped onto the tightrope, a hush fell over the crowd. He carried with him a 40-foot-long balance bar that weighed 39 pounds. When he finally stepped foot on the Canadian side, a huge cheer arose from the crowd. Then they began to shout in unison, "Blondin, Blondin, Blondin . . ." Finally, Blondin held up his hand asking for the crowd's attention. He asked the crowd, "How many of you believe I can put someone on my shoulders and walk across?"

First one person shouted, "I believe" and then a second and a third, until finally the whole crowd was shouting, "We believe! We believe! We believe!"

Then Blondin shouted, "Who would like to be that someone?" All of a sudden, everyone became quiet. They all said they believed, but no one was willing to risk their lives.

Blondin pointed his finger first at one person and then another and asked, "Would you like to get on my back as I go across?"

They all said, "No!" until he came to Harry Colcord, his manager, who said, "Yes."

Colcord got on Blondin's back, and a deathly silence fell over the crowd as Blondin stepped out onto the tight rope. Carefully, step by step, Blondin made his way across. When they were about halfway across, the rope started swaying violently back and forth. Blondin broke into a desperate run to reach the first guy rope, and when he reached it and steadied himself, the rope broke.

Once more the pair swayed as Blondin again ran for the next guy rope. When they reached it, he told Colcord to get down off of his back. Blondin looked at Colcord and said, "If we are going to make it safely to the other side, you can no longer be Colcord. You have to become a part of me. You can do nothing to try to balance yourself; you have to let me do everything. If you do anything on your own, we will both die."

Colcord then got back on Blondin's shoulders, and Blondin began to walk and then he began to run down the rope to safety on the other side.[1]

1. If you were in the crowd, would you have gone with Blondin? Why or why not?

2. What steps can Christians take to act on their belief?

3. Why is it often difficult to trust and obey Christ?

In the Word

1. Read John 14:21. If we say we love God, what will be the result according to this verse?

2. Why is this such an important principle in our Christian lives?

3. Read Hebrews 5:8-10. What was the result of Jesus' obedience?

4. What can we do as a family to help one another live a more obedient Christian lifestyle?

5. Listed below are several words. With the previous Scriptures in mind, read the word and then discuss how obedience to God fits in with each area of your life.

- serving others
- parents
- sexuality
- grades

- boyfriend/girlfriend
- parties
- worship
- tithing

6. How will you show obedience to God in these areas?

Reflect and Apply

1. Discuss the statements below and how they relate to obedience to God:

- "But Samuel replied: 'Does the Lord delight in burnt offerings and sacrifices as much as in obeying the voice of the Lord? To obey is better than sacrifice, and to heed is better than the fat of rams'" (1 Samuel 15:22).

- "True knowledge of God is born out of obedience." (John Calvin)

- "We no longer need to be obedient to our parents or our government. They left us hanging out to dry." (Seventeen-year-old student, Hoover High School, Glendale, California)

- "The starting point and the goal of our Christian life is obedience." (Andrew Murray)

- "If it feels good, do it." (unknown)

- "And this is love: that we walk in obedience to his commands. As you have heard from the beginning, his command is that you walk in love" (2 John 6).

2. How do you think the standards of our society influence our obedience to God?

3. God loves you! He wants the best for you! How do you think He feels when you walk away from Him in disobedience? How would you feel if you had children who were disobedient to you as a parent?

Note
1. Jim Burns, *Uncommon Stories and Illustrations* (Ventura, CA: Gospel Light, 2008), pp. 81-82.

19

Faith

Key Verse
Now faith is being sure of what we hope for and certain of what we do not see.
HEBREWS 11:1

The Big Idea
God will help us develop our faith and step out in faith.

Focus

Read the following story, and then answer the questions that follow to start a faith conversation:

Things looked bleak for the children in George Müller's orphanage at Ashley Downs in England. It was time for breakfast, and there was no food. A small girl whose father was a close friend of Müller's was visiting in the orphanage. Müller took her hand and said, "Come and see what our heavenly Father will do."

In the dining room, long tables were set with empty plates and empty mugs. Not only was there no food in the kitchen, but also there was no money in the orphanage's account. Müller prayed, "Dear Father, we thank You for what You are going to give us to eat."

Immediately, they heard a knock at the door. When they opened it, there stood the local baker. "Mr. Müller," he said, "I couldn't sleep last night. Somehow I felt you had no bread for breakfast, so I got up at two o'clock and baked fresh bread. Here it is." Müller thanked him and gave praise to God.

Soon, a second knock was heard. It was the milkman. His cart had broken down in front of the orphanage. He said he would like to give the children the milk so he could empty the cart and repair it.

1. What does this story tell you about George Müller?

2. How is this like or unlike your experience with prayer?

3. What steps can we take in our lives to have a stronger faith?

In the Word

Read Mark 10:13-16 together, and then discuss the following questions:

1. Why do you think Jesus' disciples didn't want the children to come to Him?

2. What point was Jesus making to His disciples when He rebuked them?

3. When you picture Jesus blessing the little children (see verse 16), what comes to your mind?

4. Some of the special qualities of a small child are a trusting nature, a sense of wonder, forgiving, total dependence, frank openness and complete sincerity. How do these traits relate to faith in God?

5. Hebrews 11:1 states, "Now faith is being sure of what we hope for and certain of what we do not see." Spend a few minutes coming up with your own definition of faith. When everyone is done, share your definitions with each other and discuss.

Reflect and Apply

1. Read Matthew 14:22-33. Finish this sentence: "If I had been Peter and Jesus invited me to step out in faith from the boat to the water, I probably would have . . ."

2. In what area(s) of your life is God calling you to step out in faith?

3. What is holding you back from making this commitment to jump in the water with Jesus?

Whenever you decide to step out in faith, you need to ask (1) whether it will glorify God, (2) if it is biblical, (3) what the significant people in your life feel about it, and (4) whether you sense God's leading in it. Before you wrap up your family time, spend a few minutes praying for each other to have faith and courage to step out of the boat and follow Jesus in complete trust.

20

Spiritual Growth

Key Verse

Being confident of this, that he who began a good work in you will carry it on to completion until the day of Christ Jesus.

PHILIPPIANS 1:6

The Big Idea

Spiritual growth is not stagnant but, through the ups and downs of life, is always moving towards a closer walk with God.

Focus

It's time for a project! Grab some blank paper and colored pens or pencils and invite each family member to create a two-year spiritual-growth timeline. Use the following questions to create your timelines:

- Where and when did God seem especially close?
- What was happening in your life at that time?
- Where and when did He seem far away?
- What was happening in your life at that time?

Next, interview each other using the following questions:

1. When was the first time you remember God being present in your life?

2. When has God sustained you through a difficult time?

3. Who has been a major spiritual influence in your life?

4. Do you have a favorite verse or Bible story? If yes, what is it?

5. If you could ask God one question about spiritual growth, what would you ask?

In the Word

Read Colossians 3:1-17, and then discuss the following questions together:

1. What spiritual growth principles can you find together in this powerful passage?

2. What attributes of a new nature are found in verses 12-17?

3. How did Jesus model these attributes?

4. For each attribute you came up with, what are some ways you could live out that attribute at home, school and work?

5. Colossians 3:17 states, "Whatever you do, whether in word or in deed, do it all in the name of the Lord Jesus, giving thanks to God the Father through him." What does it mean to "do it all in the name of the Lord Jesus"?

6. Invite each family member to choose one attribute of the new nature that he or she desires to work on this week. What are some specific ways that you will work on developing that attribute?

Reflect and Apply

1. What is the difference between salvation and spiritual growth?

2. How does Philippians 1:6 relate to spiritual growth?

3. If someone is feeling dry spiritually and they say they feel far from God, what advice would you give them?

4. Take another look at your spiritual-growth timelines. What causes growth in your spiritual life?

5. Is there anything wrong with a chart that looks like a roller coaster?

6. How can even the difficult times be times of growth?

21

The Will of God

Key Verse
Delight yourself in the Lord and he will give you the desires of your heart.
PROVERBS 37:4

The Big Idea
*The Scriptures are filled with God's will for our lives. As we follow Him daily,
He will provide guidance and direction because He loves us.*

Focus

Invite each family member to come up with a list of 10 "I am"s. (Example: I am a student, I am a Christian, I am a daughter/son, I am a softball player, and so forth.) When everyone is done, share your lists!

In the Word

It can sometimes be difficult to know the will of God for our lives. However, it can be done! Four ways that God reveals His plans are through (1) the Bible, (2) the counsel of others, (3) prayer, and (4) circumstances. Keeping this in mind, get into the Word and discuss the following questions together:

The Bible
1. Read Psalm 119:105. How does the psalmist describe the Word of God?

2. Why is the Bible our authority when it comes to knowing God's will?

3. As we read and study the Bible, we can know how God wants us to live in many situations. As a family, take turns reading the following verses out loud, and then discuss what command each gives that reveals God's will for our lives:

- James 1:26
- Matthew 6:33
- Exodus 20:12
- Exodus 20:14-15

- 1 Corinthians 6:19-20
- 1 Thessalonians 5:18
- Romans 12:1-2
- Matthew 22:37

Counsel

1. The Bible does not deal with every situation. When Scripture is silent on a subject, we look to other sources of wisdom to find out the will of God for our lives. Read Proverbs 20:18 and 11:14. What do these verses recommend?

2. To whom can you go for sound, solid advice? Have each family member brainstorm a top-5 list.

3. Why is it so important to seek the advice of someone you respect?

Prayer

1. Read James 1:5-8 and Philippians 4:6 together. What does Paul suggest you do instead of worrying about God's will?

2. According to Philippians 4:7, what will be the results of following Paul's instructions?

3. What are some specific areas in your life that you should be praying about?

Circumstances

1. Read Proverbs 3:5-6 and 16:9. Why do you think some people might call the wisdom in these verses the "open door/closed door" method of figuring out God's will?

2. What are some circumstances over which you had no control that you believe God used to lead you to do His will?

Reflect and Apply

1. Does God have the perfect job or the perfect person to marry picked out for us?

2. Sometimes we make a wrong decision. How does that fit into God's will?

3. Do you think there is ever more than one option that fits into God's will?

4. Read Matthew 6:25-34: Complete this sentence: "When I hear the phrase, 'Therefore I tell you, do not worry about your life,' I feel . . ."

5. Complete this statement: "The hardest thing for me in seeking God's kingdom and will first is . . ."

Invite each family member to name an issue or area in his or her life in which he or she is seeking God's guidance (for example, dating a non-Christian or choosing a church). Using the roadmap for finding God's will as explored in the "In the Word" section (Bible, counsel, prayer, circumstances), spend time as a family seeking God's will for each situation.

22

Jesus

Key Verses
Jesus answered, "I am the way and the truth and the life. No one comes to the Father except through me. If you really knew me, you would know my Father as well. From now on, you do know him and have seen him."

JOHN 14:6-7

The Big Idea
The life and ministry of Jesus Christ are the most powerful and influential elements of our Christian lives.

Focus

Read the following story aloud, and then use the questions to start a faith conversation:

> Here is a man who was born in an obscure village, the child of a peasant woman. He grew up in another village. He worked in a carpenter shop until He was 30, and then for three years He traveled the country preaching. He never wrote a book. He never held an office. He never owned a home. He never had a family of His own. He never went to college. He never traveled more than 200 miles from the place where He was born. He never did one of the things that usually accompany greatness. He had no credentials but Himself.
>
> While still a young man, the tide of popular opinion turned against Him. His friends ran away. One of them denied Him. He was turned over to His enemies. He went through the mockery of a trial. He was nailed upon a cross between two thieves. His executioners gambled for the only piece of property He had on earth while He was dying. When

He was dead He was taken down and laid in a borrowed grave through the pity of a friend.

Nineteen centuries have come and gone, and today He is the centerpiece of the human race and the leader of the column of progress. I am far within the mark when I say that all the armies that ever marched, and all the navies that were ever built, and all the parliaments that ever sat, and all the kings that ever reigned, put together have not affected the life of man upon this earth as has that one solitary life.

1. How do you feel when you read about the effect of Jesus' life on our world?

2. Why do you feel this way?

In the Word

Now get into the Word and discuss the following questions together:

1. Read Matthew 9:6, John 14:6, John 10:30 and Revelation 1:8. What important truth does Jesus say about Himself in each verse?

2. What or who would the world say is the way, the truth and the life?

3. If you had one question about the claims of Jesus, what would it be?

4. Read Isaiah 42:1-9, John 10:11-16 and Philippians 2:5-11. What image of Christ do you find in each of these passages?

Reflect and Apply

1. What important message is found in Hebrews 2:17-18 and 4:15?

2. What does "Jesus is fully God and fully human" mean to you?

3. What are three specific needs you have that Jesus can understand?

4. Which of Jesus' claims about Himself relates to your needs?

As a family, offer prayers of petition, asking Jesus to be who He is in these areas of need.

23

The Holy Spirit

Key Verse

But I tell you the truth: it is for your good that I am going away. Unless I go away, the Counselor (Holy Spirit) will not come to you; I will send him to you.

JOHN 16:7

The Big Idea

God sent the Holy Spirit to empower believers with guidance, revelation, power and conviction.

Focus

Read the following story, and then use the questions to start a faith conversation.

A farmer and his wife had eked out a meager living in the dusty panhandle of Texas for 30 years when an impeccably dressed man in a three-piece suit and driving a fancy car came to their door. He told the farmer that he had good reason to believe there was a reservoir of oil underneath his property. If the farmer would allow the gentleman the right to drill, perhaps the farmer would become a wealthy man. The farmer stated emphatically that he didn't want anyone messing up his property and asked the gentleman to leave.

The next year, about the same time, the gentleman again returned with his nice clothes and another fancy car. The oilman pleaded with the farmer, and again the farmer said no. This same experience went on for the next eight years. During those eight years, the farmer and his wife struggled to make ends meet. Nine years after the oilman first visited, the farmer came down with a disease that put him in the hospital. When the gentleman arrived to plead his case for oil, he spoke to the farmer's wife. Reluctantly, she gave permission to drill.

Within a week huge oil rigs were beginning the process of drilling. The first day nothing happened. The second day was filled with only disappointment and dust. But on the third day, right about noon, black bubbly liquid began to squirt up in the air. The oilman had found black gold, and the farmer and his wife were instantly millionaires.

You have a reservoir of power in your life. If you are a Christian, the Holy Spirit works in your life. The Holy Spirit will empower you to live life on a greater level, but you've got to tap into His power source, just like the farmer needed to drill for oil.

1. How does the Holy Spirit of God empower believers to live the Christian life?

2. How does this story relate to your own need to tap into God's power?

In the Word

Now get into the Word and discuss the following questions together.

1. Read John 16:5-16. Who is the Holy Spirit?

2. Who does Jesus call the Holy Spirit in verse 7? What is significant about the name that Jesus gives the Holy Spirit in this verse?

3. In verses 7-8, what did Jesus say the Holy Spirit would do when He arrived?

4. According to verses 13-14, how would the Holy Spirit guide believers? What else would He do?

5. In order to have the power of God working in our lives, we must surrender and submit ourselves to the control of the Holy Spirit of

God. Read John 14:16-18. What does Jesus say He will ask the Father to give to those who love and obey Him?

6. What is His promise in verse 18?

7. Read 1 Corinthians 3:16. How can this verse give you encouragement?

8. Read 1 Corinthians 6:18-20. How can this help you understand in greater detail the indwelling of the Holy Spirit?

9. One of the last known sentences out of Jesus' mouth is found in Acts 1:8. What is the promise for us in this verse?

10. Read Ephesians 1:13. Why is this an important verse for your spiritual life?

Take a moment to read the following prayer aloud with your family:

Spirit of the living God,
Take control of me;
Spirit of the living God,
Take control of me;
Spirit of the living God.
Take control of me;
Melt me! Mold me! Fill me! Use me!

Reflect and Apply

1. In Matthew 5:6, Jesus says, "Blessed are those who hunger and thirst for righteousness, for they will be filled." What does this tell us that we must to do to prepare our hearts for the guiding and empowering of the Holy Spirit? How does it feel to know God can actually dwell within you?

2. In Romans 12:1, Paul writes, "Therefore, I urge you, brothers, in view of God's mercy, to offer your bodies as living sacrifices, holy and

pleasing to God—this is your spiritual act of worship." What does this tell us we must do regarding our wills to receive the power of the Holy Spirit?

3. First John 1:9 states, "If we confess our sins, he is faithful and just and will forgive us our sins and purify us from all unrighteousness." What else is required of us to prepare our hearts for the Holy Spirit?

4. In Ephesians 5:18, Paul writes, "Do not get drunk on wine, which leads to debauchery. Instead, be filled with the Spirit." What command is given to believers in this verse? How can you best surrender and submit yourself to God?

5. In Galatians 5:16, Paul states, "So I say, live by the Spirit, and you will not gratify the desires of the sinful nature." What does it mean to "live by the Spirit"? What keeps believers from submitting to God's Spirit?

6. In Galatians 5:22-23, Paul states, "The fruit of the Spirit is love, joy, peace, forbearance, kindness, goodness, faithfulness, gentleness and self-control. Against such things there is no law." What is the Holy Spirit doing in your life?

Conclude by taking a moment to have each family give a brief assessment of how they are doing in each of these areas. In which areas are they doing well, and which areas need some improvement? This week, have them ask God to help them in any area that needs some work.

24

The Church

Key Verse

The body is a unit, though it is made up of many parts; and though all its parts are many, they form one body. So it is with Christ.

1 CORINTHIANS 12:12

The Big Idea

The Church is the Body of Christ made up of all believers with a variety of gifts.

Focus

Read the following story aloud, and then use the questions to start a faith conversation:

On a dangerous seacoast where shipwrecks often occur, there was once a crude little lifesaving station. The building was just a hut, and there was only one boat, but the few devoted members kept a constant watch over the sea and, with no thought for themselves, went out day and night tirelessly searching for the lost. Some of those who were saved, and various others in the surrounding area, wanted to become associated with the station and give of their time and money and effort for the support of its work. New boats were bought and new crews trained. The little lifesaving station grew.

Some of the members of the lifesaving station were unhappy that the building was so crude and poorly equipped. They felt that a more comfortable place should be provided as the first refuge of those saved from the sea. They replaced the emergency cots with beds and put better furniture in the enlarged building. Now the lifesaving station became a popular gathering place for its members, and they decorated it as a sort of club. Fewer members were now interested in going to sea on lifesaving missions, so they hired lifeboat crews to do this work. The lifesaving motif still prevailed in this club's decoration, and there was a symbolic lifeboat in the room where the club initiations were held.

About this time, a large ship was wrecked off the coast, and the hired crews brought in boatloads of cold, wet and half-drowned people. They were dirty and sick and some of them had black skin and some had yellow skin. The beautiful new club was in chaos. So the property committee immediately had a shower house built outside the club where victims of shipwrecks could be cleaned up before coming inside.

At the next meeting, there was a split in the club membership. Most of the members wanted to stop the club's lifesaving activities because they were becoming a hindrance to the normal social life of the club. Some members insisted that lifesaving was their primary purpose and pointed out that they were still called a lifesaving station. But they were finally voted down and told that if they wanted to save lives of all the various kinds of people who were shipwrecked in those waters, they could begin their own life-saving station down the coast. They did.

As the years went by, the new station experienced the same changes that had occurred in the old. It evolved into a club, and yet another lifesaving station was founded. History continued to repeat itself, and if you visit that seacoast today, you will find a number of exclusive clubs along that shore. Shipwrecks are frequent in those waters, but most of the people drown.

1. When was the lifesaving station most effective?

2. Where did the lifesaving station go wrong?

3. How is the Church like a lifesaving station?

4. What is the purpose of the Church?

5. If you don't like the Church as it is now, what alternatives do you have?

6. How can the problems that the people of the lifesaving station experienced be avoided in the Church? What should the members of the lifesaving station have done?

7. Is being a part of the Church necessary to being a Christian?

8. What can you do to help make your church a better place?

In the Word

Now get into the Word and discuss the following questions together:

1. Read 1 Corinthians 12:12-31. What different roles can people have in the Church?

2. How are the roles related to each other?

3. As a family, write a job description for your church. Rank its five major job responsibilities. Read these Bible passages to get you started: Psalms 95:6-7; 118:24; 133:1; Proverbs 18:24; 29:18; Matthew 10:7,8, 34; John 5:39; Romans 12:10; 1 Corinthians 13:3; 1 John 4:7.

4. Imagine you are applying for a job at your church. Have each family member rank his or her five top talents or skills.

5. Now match each person's skills/talents with the five most important job responsibilities of your church. Do any match?

Reflect and Apply

1. What is your first memory of church?

2. When you think of your church, what do you typically feel?

3. What is the best thing about your church?

4. What is the worst thing about your church?

5. If you were the pastor, what would you do?

6. According to 1 Corinthians 12:12-31, what are some roles you could have in your church?

7. What steps can you personally take to be more active in your church or youth group?

8. Why do we call Jesus the Head of the Church?

9. How would you describe the Church to a friend?

10. What are ways your family or you individually can improve the life and ministry of your church?

Note
1. *Ideas 5-8* (El Cajon, CA: Youth Specialties, 1980), p. 78. Used by permission.

25

Congratulations, You're Gifted

Key Verses
Now about spiritual gifts, brothers, I do not want you to be ignorant.
There are different kinds of gifts, but the same Spirit.
1 CORINTHIANS 12:1,4

The Big Idea
God has given each person unique gifts, talents and abilities.
Discovering and putting into practice the gifts God has given you will lead to a life
of fulfillment and effective leadership.

Focus

Read the following story, and then use the questions to start a faith conversation:

[The kingdom of God is] like a man going off on an extended trip. He called his servants together and delegated responsibilities. To one he gave five thousand dollars, to another two thousand, to a third one thousand, depending on their abilities. Then he left.

Right off, the first servant went to work and doubled his master's investment. The second did the same. But the man with the single thousand dug a hole and carefully buried his master's money.

After a long absence, the master of those three servants came back and settled up with them. The one given five thousand dollars showed him how he had doubled his investment. His master commended him: "Good work! You did your job well. From now on be my partner."

The servant with the two thousand showed how he also had doubled his master's investment. His master commended him: "Good work! You did your job well. From now on be my partner."

The servant given one thousand said, "Master, I know you have high standards and hate careless ways, that you demand the best and make no allowances for error. I was afraid I might disappoint you, so I found a good hiding place and secured your money. Here it is, safe and sound down to the last cent."

The master was furious. "That's a terrible way to live! It's criminal to live cautiously like that! If you knew I was after the best, why did you do less than the least? The least you could have done would have been to invest the sum with the bankers, where at least I would have gotten a little interest. Take the thousand and give it to the one who risked the most. And get rid of this 'play-it-safe' who won't go out on a limb. Throw him out into utter darkness" (Matthew 25:14-30, *THE MESSAGE*).

1. How does this story relate to using your God-given gifts for the kingdom of God?

2. Read Colossians 3:17. How does this verse relate to gifts, talents and abilities God has given you?

3. How can you use your spiritual gifts to minister to each other?

In the Word

First Corinthians 12:4-7 says, "There are different kinds of gifts, but the same Spirit. There are different kinds of service, but the same Lord. There are different kinds of working, but the same God works all of them in all men. Now to each one the manifestation of the Spirit is given for the common good." One excellent way to understand your spiritual gifts as a family is to take a spiritual gifts inventory. On the following page is a list of 27 spiritual gifts adapted from C. Peter Wagner's *Your Spiritual Gifts Can Help Your Church Grow*.[1] Have each family member write the numbers 1 to 27 on a sheet of paper. Read each item in the inventory and have them write one of the following responses for each gift:

> **Yes** = I have this gift.
> **Maybe** = It's quite possible I have this gift or will have it in the future.
> **No** = I really don't think I have the gift.
> **Unsure** = I'm not sure I know what the gift is or what it's about.

SPIRITUAL GIFTS INVENTORY

1. **Prophecy**: A special ability God gives to certain people to receive and express a direct message from Him.
2. **Service**: An ability to identify unmet needs and make use of available resources to meet those needs and help accomplish the desired goals.
3. **Teaching**: An ability to communicate information relevant to the health and ministry of others in such a way that they will learn from it.
4. **Exhortation**: An ability to give words of comfort, consolation, encouragement and counsel to others in a way that they feel helped and healed.
5. **Giving**: An ability to contribute material resources to the work of the Lord with generosity and cheerfulness.
6. **Leadership**: An ability to set goals in accordance with God's purpose for the future and communicate those goals to others in such a way that they voluntarily work together to accomplish those goals.
7. **Mercy**: An ability to feel empathy and compassion for others who are suffering and to translate that compassion into deeds that reflect Christ's love and alleviate the suffering.
8. **Wisdom**: An ability to know the mind of the Holy Spirit and have insight into how certain information may best be applied to specific needs arising among others.
9. **Knowledge**: An ability to discover, accumulate, analyze and clarify information and ideas that are pertinent to the growth and wellbeing of others.
10. **Faith**: An ability to discern the will and purposes of God for the future of His work.
11. **Healing**: An ability to serve as a human intermediary through whom God cures illnesses and restores health to others.
12. **Miracles**: An ability to serve as human intermediaries through whom God performs powerful acts that are perceived by others to have altered the ordinary course of nature.
13. **Discerning of spirits**: An ability to know whether certain behavior believed to be of God is in reality divine, human or satanic.
14. **Tongues**: An ability to speak to God in a language the person has

never learned and/or receive and communicate a message from God through a divinely anointed utterance in a language he or she has never learned.

15. **Interpretation of tongues**: An ability to interpret the message of one who speaks in tongues.

16. **Apostle**: An ability to exercise leadership over a number of churches in spiritual matters that is spontaneously recognized and appreciated by those churches.

17. **Helps**: An ability to invest the talents the person has in the life and ministry of other Christians, thus enabling the person helped to increase the effectiveness of his or her spiritual gifts.

18. **Administration**: An ability to understand immediate and long-range goals and devise and execute effective plans for accomplishing those goals.

19. **Evangelist**: An ability to share the gospel with unbelievers in such a way that they become Jesus' disciples.

20. **Pastor**: An ability to assume long-term personal responsibility for the spiritual welfare of a group of believers.

21. **Celibacy**: An ability to remain single and enjoy it—to be unmarried and not suffer undue sexual temptations.

22. **Voluntary poverty**: An ability to renounce material comforts and adopt a lifestyle equivalent to those living at the poverty level in order to serve God more effectively.

23. **Martyrdom**: An ability to undergo suffering for the faith (even to death) while displaying a joyous and victorious attitude that brings glory to God.

24. **Hospitality**: An ability to provide an open house and a warm welcome for those in need of food and lodging.

25. **Missionary**: An ability to minister one's spiritual gifts in a second culture.

26. **Intercession**: An ability to pray for extended periods of time on a regular basis and see frequent and specific answers to those prayers.

27. **Deliverance** (exorcism): An ability to cast out demons and evil spirits.

Reflect and Apply

1. Is the concept of God's having given you spiritual gifts a difficult concept to understand? Why or why not?

2. How can it be harmful to your faith to wish you had someone else's spiritual gifts?

3. How can you use your spiritual gift(s) now and in the future to serve God?

4. How will your role as a gifted Christian challenge others to use their own gifts and abilities?

Note

1. Adapted from C. Peter Wagner, *Your Spiritual Gifts Can Help Your Church Grow* (Ventura, CA: Regal Books, 1994), pp. 229-233. Used by permission.

26

Becoming Others-Centered

Key Verse
Be devoted to one another in brotherly love. Honor one another above yourselves.
ROMANS 12:10

The Big Idea
The call to Christ is the call to serve.

Focus

Use the following questions to start a faith conversation:

1. Who is the most "others-centered person" you know? What impresses you about him or her?

2. How have you been served by a person or group in the past six months? Have you experienced a significant act of kindness and service?

3. Share an experience you have had with serving someone.

In the Word

Here's an interesting statement: "If a person seeks not to receive love, but rather to give it, he or she will become lovable and will most certainly be loved in the end." That statement is a paradox! We all want to be loved; however, instead of seeking to be loved, we need to go out and love, care and serve others. In doing this we become lovable, and we experience the joy of being loved by others. There are four principles to remember in seeking to become others-centered: (1) actions speak louder than words,

(2) treat others as royalty, (3) lose yourself in service to others, and (4) realize that you are the only Jesus somebody knows. Keeping this in mind, get into the Word and discuss the following questions together:

Actions Speak Louder than Words

1. Read 1 John 3:18 together. What actions could you do to become a more others-centered person? Be specific.

2. Is it easier or harder to be others-centered in your family than with your friends? Why?

Treat Others as Royalty

1. Read Romans 12:10. What specifically can you do to treat others as royalty?

2. Name three people God is putting on your heart to treat in a special way. What do you plan to do to treat them as royalty?

Lose Yourself in the Service of Others

1. Read Luke 9:24. What did Jesus mean by this statement?

2. What is the hardest thing about being others-centered?

3. What is the best thing about being others-centered?

You Are the Only Jesus Somebody Knows

1. What does it mean that you are the only Jesus that somebody knows?

2. When you ask Jesus to come into your life, He takes up residence. You become a representative of Jesus to others. How does that make you feel?

3. How are you representing Jesus to your world?

4. What could you as a family do to better represent Jesus to the world?

Reflect and Apply

1. Jesus was called the "Suffering Servant" in the book of Isaiah. Why do you think He was called that?

2. Should we go on serving and caring for someone when there is little or no response from them? Why or why not?

3. As a family, what are 10 specific things you are doing to serve others? What are 10 more ideas you could come up with for serving together?

SPONSOR A COMPASSION CHILD

I can't think of anything more important in life than helping make an impact on the world in which we live than sponsoring a child.

Our family has sponsored a child with Compassion International for a number of years. That support of $38 a month—just $1.26 a day—covers the cost of clothing, health care and education for Ramiro Moises Santi. Our entire family looks forward to receiving Ramiro's letters, and we hope to visit him someday.

You, too, can sponsor a boy or girl who needs love, protection and encouragement. As a sponsor, you'll receive your child's photo and personal story. Your child will know you by name and appreciate your love, help and prayer. Start today by calling Compassion International's toll-free number, 1-800-336-7676, or visiting them online at www.compassion.com.

27

Serving the Poor and Oppressed

Key Verse

*The King will reply, "I tell you the truth, whatever you did for one of
the least of these brothers of mine, you did for me."*

MATTHEW 25:40

The Big Idea

*Every Christian is challenged by Jesus to serve the needs
of those who are poor and oppressed.*

Focus

Read the following poem aloud, and then use the questions to start a faith
conversation:

I was hungry . . .
    And you formed a humanities club and discussed my hunger.
Thank you.
I was naked . . .
    And in your mind you debated the morality of my appearance.
I was homeless . . .
    And you preached to me of the spiritual shelter of the love of
    God.
I was imprisoned . . .
    And you crept off quietly to your chapel in the cellar and
    prayed for my release.
I was sick . . . .
    And you knelt and thanked God for your health.
I was lonely . . .
    And you left me alone to pray for me.

1. Have you seen the Church sometimes act like the "Christian" in this poem?

2. Read Matthew 25:40. What does Jesus say about serving people in need?

In the Word

Now read Matthew 25:31-46. We can learn at least three points from this parable: (1) God wants us to help in the simple things; (2) we should give for the sake of giving; and (3) serving people means serving Jesus. As a family, discuss each of the following questions together:

God Wants Us to Help in the Simple Things

1. What are the specific actions that Jesus mentions we should do in Matthew 25:31-46?

2. What are some other simple ways to help?

3. Why would God want us to serve in the simple things?

We Should Give for the Sake of Giving

1. True giving means giving with no strings attached. What was the attitude of the people in verse 37? In verse 44?

2. What do you think it means to be generous?

Serving People Means Serving Jesus

1. What point is Jesus making in verse 40?

2. Have you ever felt as though by helping another person you were in reality helping Jesus? If yes, when and how?

3. Finish this sentence: "When it comes to the idea of serving people, I . . ."

Reflect and Apply

Read the following story aloud, and then discuss the questions that follow:

> Martin of Tours was a Roman soldier and a Christian. One cold winter day, as he was entering a city, a beggar stopped him and asked of alms; Martin had no money, but the beggar was blue

and shivering with cold, and Martin gave what he had. He took off his soldier's coat, worn and frayed as it was; he cut it in two and gave half of it to the beggar man. That night he had a dream. In it he saw the heavenly places and all the angels and Jesus in the midst of them; and Jesus was wearing half a Roman soldier's cloak. One of the angels said to him, "Master, why are you wearing that battered old cloak? Who gave it to you?" And Jesus answered softly, "My servant Martin gave it to me."[1]

1. If you could serve Jesus in any way possible, what would you do?

2. What could our family do?

3. What keeps you from committing your life to doing those acts of service?

Take a few minutes to pray for the needs of the world by name. Pray also about your family's contribution toward making a difference.

Note

1. William Barclay, *The Gospel of Matthew: The Daily Bible Study Series* (Philadelphia, PA: Westminster Press, 1975), p. 326.

28

Servant Leaders

Key Verse
I have set you an example that you should do as I have done for you.
JOHN 13:15

The Big Idea
Jesus is our example of a servant,
and we are to imitate His actions as servant leaders.

Focus

Read the following story aloud, and then use the questions to start a faith conversation:

Ever feel like a frog? Frogs feel slow, low, ugly, puffy, drooped, pooped. (I know because one told me.)

The frog feeling comes when you want to be bright but feel dumb, when you want to share but you are selfish, when you want to be thankful but feel resentment, when you want to be great but are small, when you want to care but are indifferent.

Yes, at one time or another each of us has found him- or herself on a lily pad, floating down the great river of life. Frightened and disgusted, we are too froggish to budge.

Once upon a time there was a frog. But he really wasn't a frog. He was a prince who looked and felt like a frog. A wicked witch had cast a spell on him. Only the kiss of a beautiful maiden could save him. But since when do cute chicks kiss frogs? So there he sat, an unkissed prince in frog form. But miracles happen.

One day a beautiful maiden grabbed him up and gave him a big smack. *Crash! Boom! Zap!* There he was, a handsome prince.

And you know the rest. They lived happily ever after.
What is the task of the Church? To kiss frogs, of course.

1. What is the point of this frog-kissin' story?

2. How does being a servant leader relate to this story?

In the Word

Now read John 13:1-20 together and discuss the following questions:

1. Why did Jesus wash His disciples' feet?

2. What lessons do you think Peter learned from his encounter with Jesus?

3. What is the path of blessing according to John 13:17?

4. What are some specific ways that we as a family can humble ourselves and serve others in order to make a difference in their lives?

Bring out a bucket of water and towels, and then wash each others' feet. When you're finished, answer these questions about the experience:

- What makes it uncomfortable to wash each others' feet and to have your feet washed?
- What makes it special?
- How can serving others feel similarly uncomfortable and special?

Reflect and Apply

Read the following story aloud, and then discuss the questions:

There was a soldier who was wounded in battle. A padre crept over and did what he could for him. He stayed with him when the remainder of the troops retreated. In the heat of the day he gave him water from his own water bottle, while he himself remained parched with thirst. In the night, when the chill frost came down, he covered the wounded man with his own coat, and finally wrapped him up in even more of his own clothes to save him from the cold. In the end, the wounded man looked up at the padre. Then said the wounded man, "If Christianity makes a man do for another man what you have done for me, tell me about it, because I want it." Christianity in action moved him to envy a faith which could produce a life like that.[1]

1. What is the significance of this story?

2. How does the phrase "if Christianity makes a man do for another man what you have done for me, tell me about it, because I want it" relate to being a servant leader?

3. How can our family be more effective at servant leadership?

Note

1. William Barclay, *The Letter to Romans: The Daily Bible Study Series* (Philadelphia, PA: Westminster Press, 1975), p. 148.

29

Getting Your Priorities Straight

Key Verse

*But seek first his kingdom and his righteousness,
and all these things will be given to you as well.*

MATTHEW 6:33

The Big Idea

*You can make important decisions to get your priorities in line
with God's principles.*

Focus

Read the following fun facts aloud, and then use the questions that follow to start a faith conversation:

The average person who lives to be 70 years old will spend . . .

- 20 years sleeping
- 16 years working
- 7 years playing
- 6 years eating
- 5 years dressing
- 3 years waiting for somebody
- 1½ years in church
- 1 year on the telephone
- 5 months tying his or her shoes

1. What can you do with your time today that will make a positive difference in your life?

2. What priorities could you develop to help you live life to the fullest?

3. In 1 Corinthians 10:31, Paul states, "Whether you eat or drink or whatever you do, do it all for the glory of God." What does this passage have to do with our priorities?

4. In Colossians 3:17, Paul writes, "Whatever you do, whether in word or deed, do it all in the name of the Lord Jesus." What does this passage have to do with our priorities?

In the Word

Read Matthew 6:25-34 together, and then discuss the following questions:

1. According to this passage, what is the key to putting God first in your life?

2. How can you do this?

3. Why do you think Jesus talked so much about worry while He was teaching on seeking the kingdom of God?

Reflect and Apply

Invite each family member to rank his or her top 15 priorities. These might include being physically attractive, having enough money to be happy, enjoying hassle-free family time, knowing God's will or serving others. When everyone has completed his or her list, discuss the items as a family. Now discuss the following questions:

1. Why are these your priorities? What makes them important to you?

2. How do these priorities fit with seeking God's kingdom first?

3. What might need to change?

4. How could we challenge each other to put God first?

30

Heroic Leadership

Key Verse
I can do everything through him who gives me strength.
PHILIPPIANS 4:13

The Big Idea
You can do something heroic for Jesus Christ
when you realize He is your strength.

Focus

Use the following questions to start a faith conversation:

1. Who are the 5 to 10 people on your most-admired list?

2. What do you most admire about these people?

3. Which of these people would you like to be like and why?

4. What are some action steps you could take that could help you become the kind of leader God wants you to be?

In the Word

Now discuss the following questions and get into the Word together:

1. Read 1 Samuel 17:1-58. In the conversation between David and Saul in verses 31-37, why is David confident in his fight with Goliath?

2. What motivated David to stand up to the 9½-foot giant? (Look carefully at verses 26, 36 and 45-47.)

3. Is there a "Goliath" in your life that keeps you from being more than average? If so, what is it?

4. What do you need to do to slay your Goliath?

5. Do you care about the things of the world more than you care about Jesus?

6. Do you love Jesus enough to say no to the world's standards?

7. Are you willing to lose all prestige to follow the call of God?

8. Is your goal in life to be known (or to be rich) or to follow Jesus?

9. Are you willing to pay the price of faithfulness?

10. What is your definition of a hero?

Have each member of the family write a short answer to the following question: "If you could become any type of person you wanted to become with the wave of a magic wand, who would you want to become?" Here are a few areas you and your family members might want to consider:

- Personality
- Relationship with God
- Actions
- Relationships with others
- Lifestyle
- Family relationships

Once everyone has recorded his or her answer, share what keeps each person from "going for it" when it comes to those areas. What do each of you need from your family, friends and church to not settle for mediocrity but to "go for it" for God?

Reflect and Apply

There are too many people today who settle for second-best in life. Mediocrity is all they put into life, and mediocrity is all they get out of life. Yet Paul said, "I can do all things through him who gives me strength" (Phil. 4:13). He doesn't sound like a person who chooses to be average, and we don't have to be average either. The following story illustrates this point. Read the story aloud, and then discuss the questions that follow:

An American Indian legend tells about a brave who found an eagle's nest and put one of the eggs into the nest of a prairie chicken. The eaglet hatched with the brood of chicks and grew up with them.

All his life, the changeling eagle—thinking he was a prairie chicken—did what the prairie chickens did.

He scratched in the dirt for seeds and insects to eat. He clucked and cackled. And he flew in a brief thrashing of wings and flurry of feathers no more than a few feet off the ground. After all, that's how prairie chickens were supposed to fly.

Years passed. And the changeling eagle grew very old. One day, he saw a magnificent bird far above him in the cloudless sky. Hanging with graceful majesty on the powerful wind currents, it soared with scarcely a beat of its strong golden wings.

"What a beautiful bird!" said the changeling eagle to his neighbor. "What is it?"

"That's an eagle. The chief of the birds," the neighbor clucked. "But don't give it a second thought. You could never be like him."

So the changeling eagle never gave it another thought. And it died thinking it was a prairie chicken.[1]

1. What is the tragedy of the story?

2. How does this story relate to your life?

3. How can Paul's words in Philippians 4:13, "I can do everything through him who gives me strength," change your life?

4. If you could really do anything you wanted in Christ, what would you do?

Note

1. "The Changeling Eagle," *Christopher News Notes*, no. 229.

31

Integrity

Key Verse
Blessed are the pure in heart, for they will see God.
MATTHEW 5:8

The Big Idea
God desires us to become people who are trustworthy, honest and wise.
A lifestyle of integrity leads to a fulfilled and happy life.

Focus

For this challenge, write the following statements on a separate piece of paper: "strongly agree," "agree," "undecided," "disagree" and "strongly disagree." Place each of these pieces of paper, which will serve as "signs" during this discussion, at different locations around the room. As you read the following statements, have your family members move to the sign that best represents what he or she believes.

- God wants us to always tell the truth.
- The majority of people are people of integrity.
- Pastors have more integrity than politicians.
- If a store clerk gives you back too much change and you are already at home, you should go back to the store and give the extra money to the clerk.
- It's okay to share copyrighted music.
- It's okay to speed on the freeway.

In the Word

One of the greatest compliments one could ever receive is to be called a woman or man of integrity. People of integrity can be trusted. People of integrity are honest. People of integrity have pure motives. Two people in the Old Testament who were full of integrity were Joseph and Daniel.

Joseph

In Joseph we see a person who was betrayed by his very own brothers, yet in the end, Joseph saved his family from starvation. Time after time, God abundantly blessed Joseph because of his honesty and integrity. Read Genesis 39:1-23 and answer the following questions about his story:

1. Why did Potiphar leave Joseph in charge of everything in his house and field (see vv. 1-6)?

2. What was Joseph's response to the plea of his master's wife (see vv. 7-10)?

3. What did Joseph do when Potiphar's wife cornered him in the house (see vv. 11-12)?

4. Why do you suppose Potiphar's wife lied about Joseph (see vv. 13-18)?

5. How did Joseph act in prison (see vv. 19-23)?

6. What was God's response to Joseph's integrity (see v. 21)?

Daniel

Now read Daniel 6:1-24 and answer the following questions about his story:

1. Why was Daniel distinguished above all the other leaders (see v. 3)?

2. What happened when Daniel's fellow leaders tried to find fault in him (see v. 4)?

3. What did Daniel do after King Darius signed the document (see v. 10)?

4. Why do you think the king was distressed when he heard from the other leaders that Daniel had remained faithful to God (see v. 14)?

5. What was the king's desire concerning Daniel's life in the lions' den (see vv. 16-18)?

6. What were the results of Daniel's integrity and faithfulness to God (see vv. 19-24)?

Reflect and Apply

Now it is time to take a personal integrity inventory. On a scale of 1 to 10, with 10 being the highest and 1 being the lowest, have each member of your family rate himself or herself on the following traits of integrity: honesty, purity and wisdom. Now discuss the following questions:

Honesty

1. According to Colossians 3:9-10, why should we not lie to one another?

2. How does Luke 6:31 reflect the idea of living honestly?

3. Read Hebrews 4:13. Why is it useless to try to deceive God?

Purity

1. What does Jesus say about the pure in heart in Matthew 5:8?

2. How did Paul describe those who practice impurity in Ephesians 4:18-19?

3. What suggestions does Paul give us in Galatians 5:16 and 2 Timothy 2:22 on how to live a pure life?

Wisdom

1. Read Proverbs 2:1-15. List a few of the rewards for seeking wisdom.

2. What can you personally do to develop the characteristic of wisdom in your life?

3. Read Proverbs 2:20-22. What does this verse have to say about integrity?

4. Now read Proverbs 10:9. What does this passage say about a person who walks with integrity?

5. How can we become a family of greater integrity?

32

Friendship: A Priceless Gift

Key Verse

A friend loves at all times, and a brother is born for adversity.

PROVERBS 17:17

The Big Idea

True friendship brings out the best in people.
Friendship is an incredible gift from God.

Focus

Take the following survey together, and then discuss your answers:

1. How many friends do you have?

2. Do you have friends of both sexes?

3. Do you have friends who are five years younger than you?

4. Do you have friends who are five years older than you?

5. What's the craziest thing you've done with friends?

6. Who would consider you one of their friends?

7. What are three qualities you have that make you a good friend?

8. What qualities does your best friend have?

9. Are your parents your friends? Why or why not?

10. Do you have more or fewer friends than you had one year ago?

11. Are you a good friend? Why?

12. Who are three people whom you consider to be true friends? Why?

13. Who are three people with whom you would like to be better friends? Why?

In the Word

A true friend is caring and available, encouraging, willing to sacrifice, patient and a good listener. As you discuss the following questions relating to each of these areas, have your family members consider which of these qualities are their greatest strengths in a friendship and in which areas they need improvement.

A Friend Is Caring and Available
1. Read Proverbs 17:17. How does this verse explain how you should be a good friend?

2. Read Galatians 6:2. What does this verse say in terms of being a friend who cares and is willing to be available to others in need?

3. Jesus said, "Let the little children come to me, and do not hinder them, for the kingdom of heaven belongs to such as these" (Matthew 19:14). Why do you think Jesus was available even to younger brothers and sisters?

4. How can you help people by being more available?

5. Which of your friends could use an extra dose of care from you this week? What can you do to make yourself available to him or her?

A Friend Is Encouraging
1. The special friendship of David and Jonathan is one of the most inspiring stories in the Old Testament. How does 1 Samuel 20:17 relate to the area of encouragement in their special friendship?

2. According to 1 Samuel 20:42, how is the Lord involved in their relationship?

3. Would your friends call you an encouraging person? Why or why not?

4. What are three specific ways you can be more of an encouragement to your friends?

A Friend Is Willing to Sacrifice
1. Read John 15:12-13. What is your reaction to these verses?

2. What are some little everyday sacrifices that you can make to deepen a friendship?

3. How do you think this Scripture relates to Jesus being your friend?

A Friend Is Patient

1. In 1 Corinthians 13:4, Paul writes, "Love is patient." Why do you suppose patience is included as a quality of a true friend?

2. Think of a friend with whom you can be more patient. What are some goals you could set for developing a more patient attitude with him or her?

A Good Listener

1. It has been said that listening is the language of love. Who listens to you? How has his or her listening influenced your life in a positive way?

2. Is this quality a strength or a weakness in your life? If it's a weakness, how can you become a better listener?

Reflect and Apply

Conclude by using the following questions to interview each other.

Questions for the Parents

1. Who were your best friends when you were a kid?

2. Who would you consider your best friend now?

3. How did/do your friends influence your life?

4. What is a memorable experience you had with some friends?

5. True friendship is costly. What do you think it takes to develop a deeper friendship?

Questions for the Kids

1. Which of your friends have a positive influence in your life?

2. What kinds of peer pressure do a lot of your friends experience?

3. What is one situation in which you had to sacrifice in order to keep a struggling friendship going?

4. Why do you think God gives us friends?

33

The Great Commission

Key Verses

*Therefore go and make disciples of all nations, baptizing them
in the name of the Father and of the Son and of the Holy Spirit,
and teaching them to obey everything I have commanded you.
And surely I am with you always, to the very end of the age.*

MATTHEW 28:19-20

The Big Idea

*Jesus commands all believers to make disciples and
carry on the Christian faith.*

Focus

Read the following story from Matthew 28:16-20, and then use the
questions that follow to start a faith conversation:

> Then the eleven disciples went to Galilee, to the mountain
> where Jesus had told them to go. When they saw him, they
> worshiped him; but some doubted. Then Jesus came to them
> and said, "All authority in heaven and on earth has been
> given to me. Therefore go and make disciples of all nations,
> baptizing them in the name of the Father and of the Son and
> of the Holy Spirit, and teaching them to obey everything I
> have commanded you. And surely I am with you always, to
> the very end of the age."

1. How does it feel to receive good news?

2. How does it feel to receive bad news?

3. What elements of good news are in the Great Commission—Jesus' command recorded in Matthew 28:19-20?

4. How does this good news apply to you?

In the Word

After the resurrection of Jesus, His disciples returned to Galilee, where Jesus had said He would meet them. While in Galilee, He gave His disciples the Great Commission just before ascending into heaven. Each part of the Great Commission had real significance to the disciples, and has just as much relevance to us, His disciples, today. Read each of the questions below, and then discuss your responses as a family:

1. In Matthew 28:18, Jesus states, "All authority in heaven and on earth has been given to me." On what basis could Jesus give this commission?

2. In Matthew 28:19, Jesus commands, "Therefore go and make disciples of all nations." What does it mean to make disciples? How would you do that?

3. Jesus next instructs His disciples to baptize others "in the name of the Father and of the Son and of the Holy Spirit" (v. 19). What significance does baptism have for the process of making disciples?

5. Jesus also tells His disciples to teach others everything He has commanded them (see v. 20). What would this teaching include?

6. Jesus concludes by stating, "Surely I will be with you always, to the very end of the age" (v. 20). What does Jesus' continuing presence mean for our efforts at making disciples?

Reflect and Apply

Read the following story aloud and discuss the questions that follow:

Francis of Assisi was a wealthy, highborn man who lived hundreds of years ago. He felt that his life was incomplete, and even though he had more than enough wealth, he was very unhappy. One day while he was out riding, he met a leper. The leper was loathsome and repulsive in the ugliness of his disease. Yet something moved Francis to dismount and fling his arms around this person. In the arms of Francis, the leper's face changed into the face of Christ. Francis was never the same again.

Francis of Assisi spent the rest of his life serving his Lord Jesus Christ. He wrote these famous words as a prayer to God from the heart of a man who had a deep desire to be an instrument of God's will on this earth: "Lord, make me an instrument of Your peace. Where there is hatred, let me sow love; where there is injury, pardon; where there is doubt, faith; where there is despair, hope; where there is darkness, light; and where there is sadness, joy."

1. Can you think of any biblical characters with a similar story to Frances of Assisi's? Who?

2. Can you think of any modern-day people with a similar story? Who?

3. What makes this prayer of Francis of Assisi so important to all who want to follow Jesus?

4. How does Francis of Assisi's prayer fit into the Great Commission?

5. Who are three people in your life who need your love, your care and your witness for Jesus Christ?

6. What fears do people have when it comes to telling others about Jesus?

34

The Power of Affirmation and Encouragement

Key Verses

And let us consider how we may spur one another on toward love and good deeds. Let us not give up meeting together, as some are in the habit of doing, but let us encourage one another—and all the more as you see the Day approaching.

HEBREWS 10:24-25

The Big Idea

An important part of God's work on earth is to affirm, uplift and encourage others.

Focus

Have each family member finish the following sentences:

1. The most encouraging person I know is . . .

2. One of the most encouraging experiences of my life was . . .

3. I hope I can be more encouraging to others by . . .

In the Word

Read the following story aloud, and then discuss the questions that follow:

We see over and over again in the Gospels that Jesus had the power to draw out the best in people. Remember when He met a

clumsy, big-mouthed fisherman named Simon? He looked
straight into Simon's eyes and said, "So you are Simon the son
of John." Simon nodded. Then Jesus said, "You will be called
Cephas (which, when translated, is Peter)" (John 1:42). Jesus
nicknamed Simon "The Rock."

Peter's friends and family probably laughed at the new
name Jesus had given him. Apparently he had anything but a
"rock" of a personality. They would have never believed that
this uneducated fisherman would someday be a leader of the
Church.

Jesus saw beyond Peter's problems, personality quirks and
sin. Jesus turned Peter's weaknesses into strengths. He believed
in Peter, and He had the power to draw out the best in him. Peter changed. It took years, but in the New Testament we see a
man who was transformed by the power of God because Jesus
affirmed him.

1. In the same way, God affirms each of us. To affirm means to say
   positively, declare firmly or assert something to be true. What are a
   few ways God has affirmed you?

2. God also loves us. What are some specific ways that you know God
   loves you?

3. God believes in us. What do you think it means to have God believe
   in you?

4. God draws out the best in us. What positive personality trait is God
   helping you to develop?

5. Why do you think Jesus made affirmation such an important part
   of His ministry?

6. How can affirmation be a positive way to share your faith with another person?

7. What is it like to be around a person who never has anything good
   to say about others?

8. Read Hebrews 3:13. In what ways are we to encourage each other?

9. Read Hebrews 10:24-25. How can you apply the principles of encouragement found in these verses?

10. How have you been encouraged by someone this past month?

11. Why is it sometimes so difficult to give and receive encouragement within families?

Reflect and Apply

1. Finish the following sentences to have a family time of encouragement and affirmation. Invite each person to finish the following phrases to every other family member:

   - What I especially appreciate about you is . . .
   - One of my favorite memories of you and me is . . .
   - You made my day when . . .

2. How can we as a family encourage one another more?

3. What kind of encouragement could you use from your family at this time?

Positive time together is one of the greatest sources of affirmation and encouragement. Take a moment to plan a special outing together as a family sometime during the next month.

35

Sharing the Good News

Key Verse

But God demonstrates his own love for us in this:
While we were still sinners, Christ died for us.

ROMANS 5:8

The Big Idea

God's plan of salvation is woven throughout the Scriptures and
can be offered as good news to a fallen world.

Focus

Read the following story aloud, and then use the questions that follow
to start a faith conversation:

A doctor once told a little boy that he could save his sister's life
by giving her blood. The six-year-old girl was near death, a victim of a disease from which the boy had made a marvelous re-
covery two years earlier. Her only chance for restoration was a
blood transfusion from someone who had previously con-
quered the illness. Since the two children had the same rare
blood type, the boy was the ideal donor.

"Johnny, would you like to give your blood for Mary?" the
doctor asked. The boy hesitated. His lower lip started to trem-
ble. Then he smiled and said, "Sure, Doc. I'll give my blood for
my sister."

Soon the two children were wheeled into the operating
room—Mary, pale and thin; Johnny, robust and the picture of
health. Neither spoke, but when their eyes met, Johnny grinned.

As his blood siphoned into Mary's veins, one could almost
see new life come into her tired body. The ordeal was almost

over when Johnny's brave little voice broke the silence. "Doc, when do I start to die?"

It was only then that the doctor realized what the moment of hesitation, the trembling of the lip, had meant earlier. Little Johnny actually thought that in giving his blood to his sister, he was giving up his life! And in that brief moment, he had made an incredible decision!

1. What were Johnny's conditions for giving to Mary?

2. What are your conditions for giving to another person?

In the Word

Sharing the good news of Christ with others means helping them understand that they have sinned and are in need of God's forgiveness. To do this, it is helpful to explain (1) the problem of sin, (2) the consequences of sin, (3) the solution to the problem, and (4) what our response should be to that solution. Read each of the following questions, and then discuss your answers as a family:

The Problem

1. Read James 4:17 and 1 John 3:4. According to these verses, what is sin?

2. Read Genesis 3:1-7. How did sin originate?

3. Read Romans 3:23. Who has sinned?

4. Now read Romans 3:20. How do we become conscious of the fact that we have sinned?

The Result of Sin

1. Read Ephesians 2:1-2. What is the result of sin?

2. Now read Mark 7:21-23. What does sin do in our life?

3. Read Galatians 5:19-21. What does this passage state is the result of our sin?

4. Now read Romans 6:23. What do we experience as a result of sin?

5. According to Ephesians 2:8-9, is there anything we can do to "remedy" this condition?

The Solution

1. Read John 3:16. What was God's plan for sin?

2. Now read Colossians 1:21-22. What was God's remedy for sin?

3. According to 1 Peter 3:18, what was the purpose of Christ's death on the cross?

4. What makes the cross central to our salvation?

5. Could there have been another remedy to reconcile God and humankind?

Our Response and the Result

1. Look up Revelation 3:20. What should be our response to God's offer of salvation from our sins?

2. Now read John 5:24. What is the result when we do this?

3. According to 1 John 5:11-13, what is the promise and assurance that we are given?

4. What must we do to be saved?

5. What makes these Scriptures such good news?

Reflect and Apply

1. How can we use this material to benefit our lives? How can we use this material to benefit the kingdom of God?

2. The word "gospel" means "good news." What makes the gospel of Christ such good news?

3. If the gospel is such good news, why doesn't everyone accept it?

4. Read Matthew 5:13-16. In this passage, what two images does Jesus use to describe His disciples?

5. In Matthew 5:13, Jesus said, "You are the salt of the earth." Before refrigeration, salt was used to keep meat from rotting. With this in mind, what do you think Jesus meant?

6. What might cause Christians to lose their saltiness?

7. How can a Christian be a "light of the world" (v. 14)?

8. Why do you think "light" is such a common reference to Christ and those who have faith in Him?

9. Imagine if Jesus came to you today and said, "I need you. You are My only light to your family, friends and school or work. Will you shine for Me?" What would you say and do?

10. What can we as a family do to fulfill our God-given responsibilities to be salt and light in this world?

36

God and Sex

Key Verses

Then God said, "Let us make man in our image, in our likeness, and let them rule over the fish of the sea and the birds of the air, over the livestock, over all the earth, and over all the creatures that move along the ground." God saw all that he had made, and it was very good. And there was evening, and there was morning—the sixth day.

GENESIS 1:26,31

The Big Idea
God created sex and wants the best for us.

Focus

Read each of the following statements out loud and ask each family member to decide whether it is true or false. Have each person also give a reason for his or her answer.

- The Bible is old-fashioned and out of date on the subject of sex.
- Sex before marriage is a sin.
- The Bible says sex is very good.
- Christians should avoid sex.
- Young people don't have a good understanding of sex and sexuality.

Now have each member finish this sentence: "I think God views sex as . . ."

In the Word

Now discuss the following questions and get into the Word together:

1. Knowing and understanding what God says about sex leads to wholeness in our sexuality. Read Genesis 1:26,31 and 2:18-25. How do these verses describe humankind?

2. Read Genesis 2:18. What is God's plan for humankind?

3. Now read Genesis 2:24-25. What is God's ideal for the sexual relationship between a husband and wife?

4. If God created sex and He sees it as very good, why would He ask us to wait until marriage to have sex?

5. Why do you think some people look down on sexuality? Why do you think some people overemphasize sexuality?

6. Read Hebrews 13:4. Why do you think God is so intense about this subject?

Conclude by having each person sum up in one sentence God's view of him or her and sexuality.

Reflect and Apply

1. In Philippians 2:3-4, Paul writes, "Do nothing out of selfish ambition or vain conceit, but in humility consider others better than yourselves. Each of you should look not only to your own interests, but to the interests of others." What is the main idea of this passage?

2. How does this idea relate to our sexuality?

3. In Psalm 51:10, the psalmist writes, "Create in me a pure heart, O God, and renew a steadfast spirit within me." What is the main idea of this verse?

4. How does this idea relate to our sexuality?

5. How are your ideas about sex different from God's?

6. Given what you know about God's view of and plan for sex, how do you think your understanding should change?

37

The Sexual Purity Challenge

Key Verses

Flee from sexual immorality. All other sins a man commits are outside his body, but he who sins sexually sins against his own body. Do you not know that your body is a temple of the Holy Spirit, who is in you, who you have received from God? You are not your own; you were brought for a price. Therefore honor God with your body.

1 CORINTHIANS 6:18-20

The Big Idea

Teens need to commit their bodies to God and refrain from sexual intercourse until marriage.

Focus

For this challenge, put signs that read "agree" and "disagree" on opposite walls of the room. As you read the following statements, have your family members move to the sign that best represents what he or she believes.

1. If you are really in love, it's okay to have premarital sex.

2. If you're not ready for marriage, you're not ready for sexual intercourse.

3. Premarital sex bases a relationship on physical aspects.

4. If you're pretty sure you're going to get married to the person, premarital sex is okay.

5. Premarital sex offers a false sense of intimacy.

6. People who have premarital sex are likely to cheat on their spouses after they are married.

7. Having premarital sex can have physical, emotional and psychological consequences.

8. Sex is the main way to show someone that you truly love him or her.

9. Couples—married or just dating—need to have sex to release sexual tension.

10. A person shows that he or she values and cares for you by having sex with you.

11. Having premarital sex will impact your future relationships.

12. It's important to have sex before you are married to make sure you are sexually compatible.

In the Word

When it comes to avoiding sexual immorality and remaining pure, the Bible gives us several guidelines that we should follow: (1) honor God with your body, (2) renew your mind for good, (3) turn your eyes from worthless things, and (4) guard your heart above all else. Read each of the following questions, and then discuss your answers as a family:

Honor God with Your Body

1. In 1 Corinthians 6:13, Paul writes, "The body is not meant for sexual immorality, but for the Lord, and the Lord for the body." Read 1 Corinthians 6:18-20. Why do you think the Bible tells us to "flee sexual immorality"?

2. How does this verse relate to the opposite sex?

3. According to verse 20, what is our response to the sacrificial love of Christ?

Renew Your Mind for Good

1. In Romans 12:2, Paul states, "Do not conform any longer to the pattern of this world, but be transformed by the renewing of your mind. Then you will be able to test and approve what God's will is—his good, pleasing and perfect will." With this verse in mind, how does the concept of GIGO (Garbage In/ Garbage Out) work in the area of our sexuality?

2. If you apply this verse to your life, what are the good consequences?

Turn Your Eyes from Worthless Things

1. In Matthew 6:22, Jesus says, "Your eye is a lamp that provides light for your body. When your eye is good, your whole body is filled with light." What makes your eyes such a powerful influence for good and bad when it comes to purity?

2. What can you specifically do with your eyes when it comes to sexually impure materials?

Guard Your Heart Above All Else

1. Proverbs 4:23 states, "Guard your heart above all else, for it determines the course of your life." What are practical ways to guard your heart for good?

2. According to this verse, how important is it to guard your heart? What could be the negative consequences of an unguarded heart?

Reflect and Apply

As a family, consider making a commitment to the following Purity Code. Discuss the pros and cons of making this commitment and then, if your family members are ready to commit to living by the Code, pray together and sign the commitment pledge.[1]

WHERE PARENTS GET REAL ANSWERS

*Do you not know that your body is a temple of the Holy Spirit,
who is in you, whom you have received from God? You are not your own;
you were bought at a price. Therefore, honor God with your body.*

1 CORINTHIANS 6:19-20

The Purity Code Pledge

In honor of God, my family, and my future spouse,
I commit my life to sexual purity.

This involves:

· Honoring God with my body.
· Renewing my mind for the good.
· Turning my eyes from worthless things.
· Guarding my heart above all else.

_____   _____

Signature   Date

Now discuss the following questions:

1. Now that you have looked at the Purity Code, what is your response?

2. Why do you think a lot of people reject the biblical mandate to be sexually pure?

3. What makes this way of life the best and most effective way to do relationships?

You may want to have a special time of celebration or even purchase a symbol of remembrance to signify this very important decision. (Some people choose a purity ring as a symbol of their commitment.)

Note

1. For more information on the Purity Code, see the Pure Foundations series of books created by Jim Burns. These books and CDs are for parents and students of all ages to listen to together (there is also a small-group curriculum for parents). The Pure Foundation series is available online at www.homeword.com.

Drugs and Alcohol

Key Verse

I put this in human terms because you are weak in your natural selves.
Just as you used to offer the parts of your body in slavery to impurity and to
ever-increasing wickedness, so now offer them in slavery to righteousness.
ROMANS 6:19

The Big Idea

Drugs and alcohol can have dangerous effects on the body.
Christians are to honor God with their bodies.

Focus

Invite each family member to finish the following sentences to start a
faith conversation:

- My perfect day—a day that would make me the happiest and
  that would make me feel my best—would be . . .
- I feel good physically when . . .
- I feel good mentally when . . .
- I feel good spiritually when . . .
- If I'm feeling low, three things that help me feel better are . . .
- I get the most joy in my life from . . .

Now take the following quiz together. If you're up for making it a real
competition, make sure there's a prize for the winner!

1. Heavy drinking of alcohol over a long time can cause damage to
   which of the following?

   a. the brain
   b. the liver

c. the heart
d. a, b and c

2. What is the number one drug problem among young people?

a. crack
b. alcohol
c. tobacco

3. Which of the following has as much alcohol as 1 ounce of whiskey?

a. 12 ounces of beer
b. 8-ounce glass of wine
c. 12-ounce wine cooler
d. a, b and c

4. Which of the following statements are true, and which ones are false?

a. Alcoholism is the same as being drunk.
b. A person who is an alcoholic can control the urge to drink.
c. After drinking, people often say or do things they wouldn't normally say or do.
d. Alcohol is a drug.
e. Long-term alcohol abuse can shorten a person's life.
f. A child of an alcoholic parent is less likely to abuse alcohol.

5. What are two ways alcohol affects the body?

6. What are two of the main reasons that young people drink alcohol?

In the Word

We all like to feel good about ourselves and about life, and we try all kinds of things to feel good. We do things we like, buy things we like, spend time with people we like. And let's be frank: Drugs and alcohol can make you feel good—at least for a while. But that feeling isn't true joy and it doesn't last. On top of that, drugs and alcohol can have negative effects on our bodies and minds. If you haven't approached this subject with your kids, today's study in the Word will provide you with a great opportunity to do so.

1. Read 1 Corinthians 6:19-20. How does this passage describe the body of a Christian? What does Paul say we are to do with our bodies?

2. Now turn to 1 Corinthians 9:26-27. What point is Paul making in this passage?

3. Read 1 Thessalonians 5:23. What does Paul say we are to do in this verse?

4. How are you doing in honoring God with your body?

5. What is one thing can you do to begin honoring God with your body?

6. How do drug and alcohol use relate to God's commands to care for your body?

7. How does peer pressure or the pressure to conform relate to drug and alcohol use?

8. How does a low self-image relate to drug and alcohol use?

9. Who would you go to for help if you saw yourself sinking into problems with drugs or alcohol?

Reflect and Apply

Conclude by discussing the following information. Explain that when people use drugs and alcohol, they stop learning how to cope with stress properly. At whatever age they started putting a chemical into their systems to make them feel good and deaden their pain, that is the age at which they quit coping with stress properly. People tend to change in four stages:

1. They begin with the *experimental* stage, where they try out using drugs or alcohol.

2. They then move to the *social use* stage, which leads to regular use with a high tolerance for drugs.

3. After this, they move to *dependency* (daily preoccupation), which includes use of harder drugs, a higher usage per week, and changes in behavior (such as getting lazy and letting grades drop).

4. Finally, they move to *addiction* (harmful dependency), which includes preoccupation with getting high, a loss of control, violation of their value systems and moving from one peer group to another.

Keeping this information in mind, discuss the following questions as a family:

1. Do you know anyone who has started down the road to chemical dependency?

2. Given the information we've learned in this study, what might you do to help?

3. What are some healthy ways you can feel good about yourself?

4. What can your family do to help you feel good about yourself and stand strong against temptation?

Quiz Answers
1. **D.** Alcohol can kill cells and weaken these organs.
2. **B.** More than half of all junior and senior high school students have tried alcohol.
3. **D.** Each has about the same amount of alcohol.
4a. **False.** A person can drink and get drunk but not be an alcoholic.
4b. **False.** An alcoholic is not in control of his or her drinking.
4c. **True.** As a person drinks more and more, he or she loses control of some faculties.
4d. **True.** A drug is a psychoactive substance that speeds up or slows down a person's body. Alcohol slows it down.
4e. **True.** Long-term drinking can cause fatal diseases.
4f. **False.** Alcoholism tends to run in families.
5. Alcohol slows down a person's brain and bodily control.
6. Peer pressure, to declare their independence, to have more fun, to combat loneliness, to reduce anxiety and fear, and so forth.

39

The Fight for Control

Key Verse

Do not get drunk on wine, which leads to debauchery.
Instead, be filled with the Spirit.

EPHESIANS 5:18

The Big Idea

When making a choice to use or not use drugs or alcohol,
teens need to first ask, "Who's in control?"

Focus

For today's challenge, read each of the statements below and ask your family members to choose whether using drugs or alcohol is (a) acceptable in the situation, or (b) not acceptable in the situation. After the family members state their positions, have them explain why they chose that particular response.

1. Your sister and her friend pick you up from a party, and her friend offers you a cold beer for the trip home.

2. At a party, the gang gets into the parents' liquor cabinet. Everyone starts drinking out of a bottle of vodka.

3. You are at school, between classes, and someone asks you to walk into the bathroom to smoke a joint.

4. A boy you know says he snuck some of his mother's tranquilizers out of the medicine cabinet. He asks you to meet him after school to take them.

5. Your parents take you out to a nice dinner at a local club. Your dad orders everyone something to drink and tells you it's okay for you to have one.

6. One of the high school seniors offers to give you a ride home and tells you he has some crack that is pure and expensive.

7. On a fishing trip, you go up the river with your brother. You are in the middle of the forest, and he says that since no one is around you can have a beer.

8. At one of the local hangouts, a friend says she has some bottles of cough syrup. If you drink it, she promises you will feel as though you are in another world.

In the Word

Now discuss the following questions and get into the Word together:

1. Read Romans 8:5-8 and 1 Corinthians 6:12. Do these Scriptures support the position that (1) people should never touch drugs or alcohol, (2) people should be able to use drugs or alcohol, but not in excess, or (3) people have the right to use drugs or alcohol as much as they want?

2. What do Ephesians 5:18 and 1 Peter 4:7 say about using substances such as drugs and alcohol?

3. What does 2 Peter 1:5-9 say about exhibiting self-control in our behaviors?

4. Do you think a person can be controlled by the Holy Spirit and drink or get high at the same time? Why or why not?

5. Do you think that most teenagers are able to control drinking and/or drugs? Why or why not?

6. How would a person know if he or she had passed the point of being in control?

Reflect and Apply

1. Do you know anyone who has had negative experiences with drugs and/or alcohol? If so, how has this affected your own thoughts about the use of drugs or alcohol?

2. Imagine for a moment that you were at a party and you noticed that your best friend was getting drunk. What advice would you give to him or her?

3. Do you agree or disagree with the following statement: "Never put something in your body when you do not know how it will affect you"? Give a reason for your answer.

4. Is it consistent for parents to have alcohol in their homes and forbid their children from drinking? Why or why not?

5. Should you attend a party where you know drugs and alcohol will be prevalent? Why or why not?

6. A Japanese proverb states, "First the man takes a drink, then the drink takes a drink, then the drink takes a man." What's your personal philosophy on drug and alcohol use?

40

Substance Abuse

Key Verses

*"Which of these three do you think was a neighbor to the man who
fell into the hands of robbers?" The expert in the law replied,
"The one who had mercy on him." Jesus told him, "Go and do likewise."*

LUKE 10:36-37

The Big Idea

*When a friend or family member has a potential drug or alcohol problem,
it affects more than one person. You can make some important decisions
even if your friend or family member chooses not to change.*

Focus

Use the following questions to start a faith conversation:

1. If a friend drinks and doesn't want to quit, which philosophy is the
   best idea?

   · Back off the friendship.
   · Confront the issues.
   · Preach at him or her.
   · Encourage him or her to get some help.

2. Do you agree or disagree with the following statement: "People with
   drinking or drug problems sometimes don't need our help"? Give a
   reason for your answer.

3. What do you think causes a person to abuse drugs or alcohol?

In the Word

If you're familiar with the story of the Good Samaritan, you'll remember that Jews and Samaritans did not like each other. In fact, Jews were so disgusted with Samaritans that they would walk hundreds of miles out of their way so that they wouldn't have to walk through Samaria. But in the following story that Jesus told, it was the Samaritan man who went out of his way and spent his time and money to help an injured Jewish man. Read this story aloud, and then discuss the questions that follow:

> A man was going down from Jerusalem to Jericho, when he was attacked by robbers. They stripped him of his clothes, beat him and went away, leaving him half dead. A priest happened to be going down the same road, and when he saw the man, he passed by on the other side. So too, a Levite, when he came to the place and saw him, passed by on the other side. But a Samaritan, as he traveled, came where the man was; and when he saw him, he took pity on him. He went to him and bandaged his wounds, pouring on oil and wine. Then he put the man on his own donkey, brought him to an inn and took care of him. The next day he took out two denarii and gave them to the innkeeper. "Look after him," he said, "and when I return, I will reimburse you for any extra expense you may have" (Luke 10:30-35).

1. The Bible is full of verses that remind us that we need to help those in need. But the story of the Samaritan goes even further. What lesson can we take away from this story about helping others?

2. Why is it strange that both the priest and the Levite passed the injured man by, not only ignoring him, but also actually walking on the other side of the street to get farther away from him?

3. What steps did the Samaritan take to help the injured man?

4. What was the Samaritan's attitude about helping the injured Jew?

5. How can we relate this passage to loving friends or family members who are dealing with drug or alcohol abuse?

6. What would showing mercy to a friend or family member struggling with substance abuse look like? What actions would show mercy?

Reflect and Apply

Read the following illustration aloud, and then discuss the questions that follow:

> Living with an alcoholic or drug addict is often compared to living with an elephant in your living room. The family washes and feeds the elephant. They clean up its messes, but seldom do they discuss the real problem. Sometimes they erupt with anger, but most of the time they act as if it is fairly normal to have an elephant in their living room.

1. What do you think of this illustration?

2. Does our family have any elephants in the living room?

3. If yes, what is it and what can we do about it?

If your family members have indicated that addiction is an issue in your family, ask them to offer some suggestions about what you can do to change the situation (seeking help from a qualified counselor would be a good item to have in the list). Now take a few minutes to pray together about these issues. If addiction is not a problem for your family, take a few minutes together to offer a prayer of thanksgiving for each person.

41

Your Mind and the Media

Key Verse

Whatever is true, whatever is noble, whatever is right,
whatever is pure, whatever is lovely, whatever is admirable—
if anything is excellent or praiseworthy—think about such things.

PHILIPPIANS 4:8

The Big Idea

Whatever you put into your mind will eventually come out.
Put garbage in, garbage comes out.

Focus

Use the following questions to start a faith conversation:

1. How would you describe the kind of food you eat most often? (Healthy? Sugary? Fast food? Grown in the ground? Found in a can?)

2. How would you describe the kind of music you listen to the most often? (Uplifting? Glorifying God? Encouraging? Negative? Destructive?)

3. How would you describe the kind of movies and TV shows you watch the most often? (Educational? Encouraging? Positive? Mental escape? Violent?)

4. How would you describe the kind of books and magazines you spend the most time reading? (Positive? Informational? Pleasing to God? Time-wasters? Trashy? Gossipy? Lowering your self-esteem?)

5. How would you describe the kind of websites you most often visit? (School-related? Helping you connect with others? Inspirational? Pornographic? Gossip sites? Distractions from reality?)

In the Word

Read Philippians 4:4-9, and then discuss the following questions as a family:

1. What is some of the advice Paul gives to the Philippians?

2. Is it easy for you to "not be anxious about anything" but to "present your requests to God" (verse 6)? How do you deal with difficult times?

3. Are you currently filling your mind and life with things that are noble, true, pure and admirable images, songs, people and experiences? Why or why not?

4. God is clear: Our mind matters to Him, and we have to be proactive in keeping it pure. We keep it pure by avoiding negative influences and constantly renewing our minds. What are some common negative influences?

6. Why are people drawn to negative influences, even when they know that those influences are bad for them?

7. Read Romans 12:2 and Colossians 3:1-4. How can we constantly renew our mind?

8. What does "set your minds on things above" mean?

9. Do you think that it is important to consider the things that you see, hear and read? Why or why not?

10. How can your choices about what you read, watch and listen to impact your faith? Your attitude? Your actions?

Reflect and Apply

Read the following scenarios aloud, and then brainstorm together what you would say to each person:

- **Scenario One:** Your 12-year-old brother, Seth, has recently started listening to certain kinds of rap music with lyrics that condone drug and alcohol use, excuse violence against other people and portray women in a derogatory manner. What would you say to him?

- **Scenario Two:** Your mom is addicted to watching *The Real Housewives of Orange County*. She closely follows all the drama and participates in a number of blogs about the show. You often hear her comment about what nice clothes, cars and jewelry all the women have. What would you say to her?

- **Scenario Three:** Your best friend is consumed with celebrity gossip and constantly surfs websites and blogs to hear the latest news, see the newest fashions and follow the star trends. You've noticed that she's been complaining that she's fat, even though she is in great shape, and has said some underage stars who have been in the news for their misbehavior "really aren't that bad." What would you say to her?

Conclude by sharing some examples of celebrities you've heard about who live out the "garbage in, garbage out" lifestyle. Discuss what you as a family can do to help each other consume good things, rather than garbage.

42

Contemporary Christian Music

Key Verse

Turn my eyes away from worthless things; preserve my life according to your word.

PSALM 119:37

The Big Idea

Young people need to be selective in viewing movies and TV programs.

Focus

In the 1950s and 1960s, many churches in America began to seek new ways of reaching youth and bringing them into their congregations. Many in the church felt that young people perceived church to be a stuffy, structured and dull place and that they needed to change this impression. Many congregations began adopting a different style of worship, shifting from some of the older hymns to more contemporary-sounding songs. Over time, Christian rock bands began to form that performed concerts much like their secular counterparts. Today, churches such as Hillsong in Australia have popularized contemporary praise music, which are typically led by a worship band in a church. All of these shifting trends have, of course, led people to view contemporary Christian music differently. Use the following questions to discuss this idea with your family:

1. When you think of "Christian music," what jumps into your mind?

2. Do you choose to listen to Christian music? Why or why not?

3. What is your favorite Christian song? What do you like about it?

4. What is your favorite secular song? What do you like about it?

5. In what ways are Christian musicians different than secular musicians? In what ways are they the same?

6. In Ephesians 5:18-19, Paul writes, "Be filled with the Spirit, speaking to one another with psalms, hymns, and songs from the Spirit." Some have claimed that the contemporary music heard in churches today distracts people from worshiping God. Do you agree or disagree?

7. What are the benefits of filling your mind with music that focuses on God and what He has done for us?

8. Could contemporary Christian music ever be a negative influence? If so, in what ways?

In the Word

Read Psalm 150, and then discuss the following questions together:

1. Although Psalm 150 was written thousands of years ago, its message still applies today. Think about the world in which you live (the different types of people, places, things, situations, and so forth). For what are you to praise God?

2. You may not have a harp or lyre lying around, but what are some other ways in which you can praise God?

3. In what situations are we to praise God?

4. In what settings are we to praise God?

5. What other guidelines does this Scripture give for praising God?

6. Read 1 Peter 4:12-14. What else does the Bible say that we ought to praise God for?

Reflect and Apply

Conclude by reading the following statements out loud. Ask your family members to consider each statement and then indicate whether they agree, disagree or are unsure about it. Have each person briefly share why he or she gave a particular response.

1. I love the music at our church.

2. Any kind of contemporary Christian music is fine.

3. Contemporary Christian music is a poor substitute for good secular music.

4. I'm concerned about the music on secular radio.

5. The lyrics in songs have little or no influence on my actions.

6. Our family totally disagrees on our views of music.

7. Psalm 150 is an example of why contemporary Christian music is a good idea.

43

Discretionary Viewing

Key Verse
Turn my eyes away from worthless things; preserve my life according to your word.
PSALM 119:37

The Big Idea
Young people need to be selective in viewing movies and TV programs.

Focus

For this challenge, begin by asking each family member to write down on a piece of paper his or her top three favorite websites, television shows and movies. When they have finished, read Paul's words in Philippians 4:8: "Finally, brothers, whatever is true, whatever is noble, whatever is right, whatever is pure, whatever is lovely, whatever is admirable—if anything is excellent or praiseworthy—think about such things." Now ask each person to consider how *God* would rate His approval of his or her favorite websites, TV shows and movies in light of this passage. Have them rank each on a scale of 1 to 10, with 1 being the least approval and 10 being the highest approval. After you have done this, ask your family members if there is anything they feel they need to change about their viewing habits.

In the Word

In Psalm 101, the writer focuses on how he can be pure and blameless, looking at "no vile thing" (verse 3). Read this psalm to your family, and then answer the questions that follow.

1. "I will be careful to lead a blameless life. . . . I will conduct the affairs of my house with a blameless heart" (v. 2). How can you lead a blameless life before the Lord?

2. "I will not look with approval on anything that is vile. I hate what faithless people do; I will have no part in it" (v. 3). How does this relate to your viewing habits and what you are putting into your mind?

3. "The perverse of heart shall be far from me; I will have nothing to do with what is evil." What does this say about choosing your friends?

4. "Whoever slanders their neighbor in secret, I will put to silence" (v. 5). What does this say about participating in gossip? Why is it important not to partake in slandering another person?

5. "My eyes will be on the faithful in the land, that they may dwell with me; the one whose walk is blameless will minister to me" (v. 6). Who will you look to as a role model and mentor in your life? Who do you know who will keep you accountable as you strive to lead a blameless life?

6. "No one who practices deceit will dwell in my house; no one who speaks falsely will stand in my presence" (v. 7). What does this tell you about the types of things that you should or shouldn't be viewing?

Reflect and Apply

1. Has Internet, TV or movies gotten in the way of family communication in the past month? If so, in what ways?

2. What bugs you most about TV, the Internet or movies?

3. What do you like best about TV, the Internet or movies?

4. What is the maximum number of hours that our family should spend watching TV or being on the Internet each day?

5. What are the acceptable movie ratings for each family member? Are the ratings different for different individuals? If so, should this be the case?

6. What television programs, websites and video games are not acceptable in our home?

7. What is one television program that the family could watch together each week?

8. What is one movie that fits biblical standards that we could watch as a family?

44

Family Roles and Goals

Key Verses

Children, obey your parents in the Lord, for this is right.
Fathers, do not exasperate your children; bring them up
in the training and instruction of the Lord.

EPHESIANS 6:1,4

The Big Idea

When biblical principles are implemented in the home,
stronger, healthier relationships are developed.

Focus

It's project time! Give each family member a blank piece of paper to create a family "coat of arms." Start by drawing a shield or breastplate shape that takes up most of the page. Then divide the space within the shield into eight sections. In each of those sections, invite family members to draw or write their answers to the following:

- Family name
- Where the family is from
- Our family's favorite meal
- Our family's favorite tradition
- Something unique about our family
- Our favorite family activity
- Our family's funniest private joke
- Draw a family portrait

When everyone is finished, share your coats of arms and discuss!

In the Word

Now get into the Word and discuss the following questions together:

1. Read Exodus 20:12. What does this passage say about children respecting their parents?

2. What does Proverbs 13:1 say about children following parents' instructions?

3. Now read Matthew 10:37-39. What does this say about the role our families play in our lives? Who should be first?

4. What does Jesus say in Matthew 18:6-7 about parents' role in raising their children?

5. Now turn to Ephesians 6:1-4. What are the children's responsibilities in a family? What are the parents' responsibilities?

6. What does 1 Timothy 5:8 say about families providing for one another?

7. Why do you think God's Word has so much to say about families?

8 Imagine a family that practices every single one of these biblical principles. What would their relationships look like?

9. Which of the biblical principles are the most evident in your family?

10. Which of the biblical principles does your family need to work on the most?

Reflect and Apply

1. What is one goal for your relationship with your family?

2. What is one spiritual goal that you have for your life?

3. How can your family help you achieve this goal?

5. What areas of your home life need the most improvement?

6. What goals would you like to set for your family?

7. What changes will have to be made to accomplish these goals?

8. What are the problems or hindrances that stand in the way of attaining these goals?

9. In your own words, describe the divine promise found in Philippians 4:19: "My God will meet all your needs according to his glorious riches in Christ Jesus." How does this promise relate to your family's goals?

45

Expressing Appreciation

Key Verse
*Therefore encourage one another and build each other up,
just as in fact you are doing.*
1 THESSALONIANS 5:11

The Big Idea
Family members need to express words of encouragement to one another often.

Focus

Use the following questions to start a faith conversation:

1. What was one special time in our family's life that stands out in your mind?

2. What do you most appreciate about your parents?

3. What do you most appreciate about your siblings (or children, if you're the parent)?

4. What is your most favorite funny family memory?

In the Word

One of the most effective ways to encourage your family (or anyone else, for that matter) is to honor them by listening. Listening is truly the language of love. Today, examine how well you and your family listen to each other by discussing the following questions:

1. Read Proverbs 12:15. According to this verse, what do wise people do?

2. According to James 1:22-25, what else must accompany listening? Why is this important?

3. Turn to Proverbs 15:31-32. What is the value in not only listening but also acting upon wise correction?

4. Mark Twain once said, "I can live two months on one good compliment." What specific thing(s) can you compliment each family member on this week?

5. How can you be more available to each family member?

6. What special thing can you do for them this week?

7. In his book *The Five Languages of Love*, Gary Chapman describes five different languages we use to express and receive love. They are: words of affirmation, quality time, receiving gifts, acts of service and physical touch. Which of these is your dominant "love language"?

8. When was a time when another family member made you feel loved?

9. How can you be more sensitive to each others' love language?

Reflect and Apply

Having a ministry of encouragement to your family is easy. Although it often doesn't come naturally, once you've made it a habit, you'll find that it's just like breathing. Here's what you can do to have a ministry of encouragement:

- Believe in your family members.
- Get tuned in to each family member's struggles and hopes.
- Be liberal with your praise for your parents and other family members. "Therefore encourage one another and build each other up, just as in fact you are doing" (1 Thess. 5:11).

Keeping this in mind, have a time of affirmation bombardment! Invite each person to write on a piece of paper three affirming comments about each family member. Then, one at a time, have the others barrage each family member with words of affirmation.

46

The Power of Being There

Key Verse

He took the children in his arms, put his hands on them and blessed them.

MARK 10:16

The Big Idea

*Family members regard your very presence
as a sign of caring and connectedness.*

Focus

Read the following story, and then use the questions that follow to start
a faith conversation:

My (Jim's) mom died a few years ago. It wasn't easy. Cancer
racked her body and we spent most of a year watching her die.

We brought Mom home from the hospital and tried to
make her as comfortable as possible, so we moved a hospital
bed into Mom and Dad's bedroom. I would often find myself
sitting on their bed while she lay in her hospital bed.

One day she was dozing and very weak, when all of a sudden she perked up and asked me, "Jimmy, where is your dad?"

"He's watching a ball game on TV. Do you need him, Mom?"

"No, not really," she replied. Then she looked up at me and
said, "You know, Jimmy, I never really liked baseball."

"You never liked baseball, Mom?" I was so very puzzled.
"Did you ever miss a little league game of mine?"

"No."

"Did you ever miss any of my Pony league, junior high or
high school games, Mom?"

Again she replied, "I don't think so."

"Mom," I continued, "you never missed a game and on top of that you never missed any of my three brothers' games either. Dad and you watch ball games all day long on TV. What do you mean you never liked baseball?"

"Jimmy, I didn't go to the games to watch baseball. I went to the games to be with you!"

I realized at that moment why this incredible woman had had such a powerful impact on my life: because she was there, even when she didn't care for the activity. Her very presence in my life was cause for great inspiration and influence.

1. Who has had the power-of-being-there influence in your life? How has your life been affected or influenced because of this person?

2. What is the best part of knowing that someone will be there for you?

3. Can you think of a story from the Bible in which Christ had a power-of-being-there influence on someone?

In the Word

When it comes to being a positive influence in your family members' lives, there are two things that you can do: (1) bless them with your presence, and (2) bless them with your affection. Keeping this in mind, discuss the following questions together:

Blessing Your Family with Your Presence

1. Read Mark 10:13-14. What did the disciples do when people brought little children to Jesus?

2. How did Jesus react to the disciples?

3. Why do you think Jesus allowed the little children to come to Him?

4. In 1 Thessalonians 2:8, Paul writes, "We loved you so much that we were delighted to share with you not only the gospel of God but our

lives as well, because you have become so dear to us." How does this verse relate to blessing your family with your presence?

5. What can you do to bless your family with your presence?

Blessing Your Family with Your Affection
1. Mark 10:16 states that Jesus "took the children in his arms, put his hands on them and blessed them." How did Jesus bless the children? How do you think hugging the children and blessing them are related?

2. UCLA researchers have found that it takes 8 to 10 meaningful touches a day for a person to feel loved. Many people are literally starved for physical attention, affection and warmth, even though they are part of a family whose members love one another. On a scale from 1 to 10—with 1 being no affection and 10 being extremely affectionate—how would you rate your family?

3. What are one or two things you can do this week to bless each family member with affection? (For example: bring Mom flowers, write an "I love you" or "I appreciate you" note, give a neck rub, hug family members without being asked.) Think of something specific to do for each family member.

Reflect and Apply

Read the story below, and then discuss the questions that follow:

My grandmother Nene was one of the major heroes of my (Jim's) life. At 87, she was losing it physically, and her mental condition had deteriorated because of Alzheimer's. Sometimes she recognized me, and sometimes she didn't. I never dreamed she would live to see our last child born, but she did. She was even able to come to the baby shower. I have a picture of Nene holding our youngest daughter, Heidi. Both have a dazed look on their faces. Nevertheless, I treasure that picture to this day.

When it was time to open the shower presents, my brother, Bill, went over to help Nene out of her chair. I happened to be walking by when he said, "Come on Nene, let's go watch Jim and Cathy open those presents for their new baby, Heidi."

Dazed and confused, she said, "Who?"

He said, "Jim and Cathy had a baby and we are going to open some gifts, come on I'll help you up."

Frustrated and in pain, she told Bill, "I can't get up. I didn't buy them a present. I'm tired, I'm old, I'm sick and I just want to die."

Bill replied, "Nene, I don't think anyone is concerned that you didn't get them a gift."

At this point I walked up to my dear, loving grandma and said, "Nene, your very presence in this room makes a difference to me. For all my life just your presence has given me strength."

Nene died shortly after the baby shower. She never really had much money, but it was never her gifts that made a difference—it was her very presence that still gives me strength today.

1. How is "being present" a gift to those you love?

2. Who has been a source of strength in your life just by their mere presence?

3. How has that person made a difference to you?

4. What prevents you from "being there" for other family members?

5. How have you experienced God's presence in your family's life?

Resolving Conflict

Key Verse

Bear with each other and forgive whatever grievances you may have against one another. Forgive as the Lord forgave you.

COLOSSIANS 3:13

The Big Idea

When biblical principles are properly applied to resolving conflict, family relationships become healthier and communication is clearer.

Focus

At one time or another, every family experiences conflict. What is important is how you as a family work together to address the issues and resolve the situation. The following questions can help you examine how you deal with problems and challenges:

1. What types of things tend to set off certain members in our family?

2. How does each person typically deal with frustration and anger?

3. Is that method generally effective? Why or why not?

4. Have you ever had a time when you said something you later regretted to a family member? How did you resolve the issue?

5. What are some things you can do to avoid conflict with others in your family?

6. Do you generally seek out conflict or avoid it?

7. Sometimes when your family is in the midst of conflict, it helps to stop and remember the good times you have had. What is one of your most special memories you have about your family?

In the Word

Jacob and Esau, twin brothers, were in conflict even before their birth. That conflict continued into their adulthood, and they didn't deal with it correctly. Eventually they did resolve their conflicts, and there are at least six actions that helped them come to a resolution. These actions will work for you as a family as well as in whatever conflict situation you encounter. Read Jacob and Esau's story in Genesis 32:1-20; 33:1-12, and then discuss the following questions:

1. The first thing Jacob did to resolve his conflict with Esau was to take the initiative in communicating his desire for resolution (see Genesis 32:3-5). Why is taking the initiative often very difficult to do?

2. Next, Jacob prayed about the problem (see Genesis 32:9-12). Why is it so easy to leave God out of the situation when we experience conflict?

3. Jacob then identified the problem and confessed his fears (see Genesis 32:11). Why is this an important step?

4. Jacob also attempted to see the problem from Esau's perspective and anticipate his possible resistance (see Genesis 32:13-20). How can this help in resolving conflicts with others in your life?

5. Next, Jacob told how he felt (see Genesis 33:3-4). Why is it important to explain your feelings to the other person when dealing with conflict?

6. Finally, Jacob took action to correct the problem and made restitution (see Genesis 33:10-11). Esau, for his part, offered his forgive-

ness and acceptance instead of seeking to get even (see Genesis 33:4,10-11). How does admitting guilt and offering forgiveness bring healing into the situation? What is the danger in not forgiving and letting go of the hurt?

7. Which of these steps is hardest for you personally? Which is hardest for your family?

8. With whom do you need to resolve a conflict right now?

9. Which of these suggestions will be especially beneficial in doing this?

Reflect and Apply

Conclude by reading the following list of issues that can easily turn a house into a war zone. After you read the list, have your family members rank their top three conflict points, with number 1 being the worst.

- Not cleaning your room
- Choice of friends
- Coming home too late
- Spending money
- Not doing chores on time
- Attending church
- Using bad language
- Not performing well in school
- Using the phone
- Clothing choices
- Hairstyle choice
- Using the car
- Sleeping habits
- Time spent on the Internet or gaming
- Movie or TV program choices
- Eating habits

1. Which of these items seem to be the biggest source of conflict in the family? Why do you think this is the case?

2. Why do you think some of these issues are so important to parents?

3. Why do parents and kids have so many conflicts?

4. What are some ways we as a family can handle our conflicts more lovingly?

Frazzled Families

Key Verse
If any of you lacks wisdom, he should ask God who gives generously to all without finding fault, and it will be given to him.
JAMES 1:5

The Big Idea
Thriving families seek God first and set their priorities by His standards. Frazzled families are unfocused and too busy to develop strong relationships with one another and with God.

Focus

Let's face it: Life sometimes gets too busy and our lives go into "overload syndrome." This means we take on more than we can handle. Using the illustration of car gears, here are the different levels at which we live our lives:

- **Park:** A time for rest and renewal and to recharge your batteries. Rest soothes, heals and gives you perspective.
- **Low:** Quality time for relationship building with family, friends and God.
- **Drive:** Uses lots of energy, but it is a productive time. This gear is needed to perform your usual daily tasks.
- **Overdrive:** Reserved for times that demand lots of effort. You can't always stay in overdrive or you'll run out of gas sooner and eventually burn up the engine.

Read each of these different levels to your family members, and then discuss the following questions:

1. Which gear do you usually find yourself in?

2. Which gear is your family usually in?

3. What are the three biggest overload factors in your life right now?

4. Sometimes life spins out of control. What do you do to get it back in perspective?

5. As a family, how can we help each other to get out of overload mode and find some peace?

In the Word

Read Matthew 22:34-40 together. In this passage, one of the Pharisees asks Jesus to explain what is the greatest commandment in the Law (the Law that God had given to the Israelites in the Old Testament). Jesus' response indicated that love was the most important commandment. Loving God and others means (1) putting God first in your life, (2) becoming others-centered, and (3) loving yourself.

Loving God Means Putting Him First

1. What does it mean to put God first in your life?

2. How often do you spend a regular time alone with God?

3. Does your family have a regularly scheduled time for family devotions and prayer? If not, what prevents you from spending a specified time with God?

4. Why is it so easy to neglect our relationships with God and our family?

5. How can putting God first in your life help your family life?

6. What advice would you give to someone who is struggling with putting God first in his or her life?

Loving Your Neighbor Means Becoming Others-Centered

1. What do you think it means to love your neighbor as you love yourself?

2. Could your family members be considered your neighbors? Why or why not?

3. What happens if you are too busy to love your neighbors?

4. What can you do to ensure that you will be in a good relationship with your family?

Loving Yourself

1. Think of someone who loves and takes care of himself or herself in a positive and healthy manner. What does this person do that demonstrates he or she has a balanced love of God, others and self?

2. What does it mean to you to love yourself?

3. How can you keep a healthy balance between loving God, others and self?

Reflect and Apply

1. What does each family member believe to be the greatest cause of stress within your family? (Too many activities? Work/school pressures? Finances? Health problems? Conflict?)

2. Read Matthew 6:33 and James 1:5. How do these verses relate to the subject of reducing stress in your life?

3. One important stress reducer is making time to talk to one another. Sharing one another's thoughts and needs builds stronger

relationships, and it lightens the load when others can share your burden and pray for you. Does your family have a regular daily time of connecting with one another in conversation, such as at dinnertime or bedtime? If not, can you schedule a regular time right now?

4. Another great stress reducer is rest and relaxation. How often does your family plan a day, evening or weekend of fun? If it is not very often, can you take time right now to plan something for the near future?

5. Do you regularly schedule time in each week for family fun and relaxation? If not, why not?

6. What activities or pressures could be lightened or dropped completely to simplify your family life?

There are times when stress is inevitable. In fact, managed amounts of stress can help us accomplish important things. The secret is in relying on the Lord to help us manage stress properly. As Paul states in Philippians 4:13, "I can do all this through him who gives me strength." Spend time in prayer for each family member, asking for God's wisdom to deal with stress.

49

The Birth of Christ

Key Verses

*But the angel said to them, "Do not be afraid. I bring you good news
of great joy that will be for all people. Today in the town of David a Savior
has been born to you; he is Christ the Lord."*

LUKE 2:10-11

The Big Idea

*The birth of Jesus Christ was a supernatural event foretold
by Old Testament prophecies. His birth shows God's love for our world
and reconciles our relationship with God.*

Focus

Read the following story, and then use the questions to start a faith
conversation:

Once upon a time, there was a colony of ants that were busy
doing whatever ants do with their lives. God wanted to tell the
ants of His love for them and His eternal home He had pre-
pared for them. What was the very best way for God to communicate to those ants? The only possible way to speak to the
ants was to become an ant and speak their language. So He did,
and they believed. The Incarnation represents the ultimate act
of God's love. God answered the question "How do you pack-
age love?" by using a stable and straw and a tiny Baby. The baby
Jesus, born in a stable, was fully human and fully God.

1. What makes this act of God a sign of deep love?

2. Why is it so difficult to comprehend God's unconditional love?

3. Read Hebrews 2:17-18. How is Jesus able to identify with you?

4. How can this Scripture help you live your Christian life?

In the Word

Read the story of the birth of Christ is Luke 2:1-20, and then answer the questions that follow:

1. What part of this story impresses you the most?

2. What events in this passage were supernatural—those events that could not have happened unless God arranged them?

3. The Old Testament contains a number of prophecies (foretelling of the future) about the birth of the Messiah. These prophecies were given to people by God hundreds of years before the birth of Jesus. Read Micah 5:2 and Matthew 2:1-6. What was the Old Testament prophecy, and what was the fulfillment?

4. Read Isaiah 7:14 and Matthew 1:23. What Old Testament prophecy was fulfilled in this case?

5. Read Matthew 1:18-25. If you were Joseph, how would you have reacted when Mary told you she was pregnant?

6. What factor(s) influenced Joseph to change his mind?

7. Now read Matthew 2:1-12. What circumstances led to the wise men visiting Jesus in Bethlehem?

8. What did they do when they arrived in Bethlehem?

9. What can you do today that is similar to what the wise men did when they saw Jesus almost 2,000 years ago?

10. What is your response to this most incredible event?

Reflect and Apply

Read the excerpt from C. S. Lewis below, and then discuss the questions that follow.

> I am trying here to prevent anyone saying the really foolish thing that people often say about Him: "I'm ready to accept Jesus as a great moral teacher, but I don't accept His claim to be God." That is the one thing we must not say. A man who was merely a man and said the sort of things Jesus said would not be a great moral teacher. He would either be a lunatic—on a level with the man who says he is a poached egg—or else he would be the devil of hell. You must make your choice. Either this man was, and is, the Son of God, or else a mad man or something worse. You can shut Him up for a fool, you can spit at Him and kill Him as a demon or you can fall at His feet and call Him Lord and God. But let us not come with any patronizing nonsense about His being a great human teacher. He has not left that open to us. He did not intend to.[1]

1. What are your thoughts about this statement made by C. S. Lewis?

2. What can your family do to make Jesus the Lord of your family?

Note

1. C. S. Lewis, *Mere Christianity* (London: HarperCollins, 1952), p. 54.

50

The Crucifixion of Jesus

Key Verses

He himself bore our sins in his body on the tree, so that we might die to sins and live for righteousness; by his wounds you have been healed.

1 PETER 2:24

The Big Idea

The Crucifixion is the condemnation of Jesus Christ as a criminal, but more importantly, it is the point in history where the sin of humanity is confronted by the love of God.

Focus

Discuss the following questions to start a faith conversation:

1. When you think of the word "sacrifice," what comes to your mind?

2. Who is someone who has sacrificed something for you?

3. When was a time when you sacrificed something for someone else?

4. What images come to your mind when you think of the sacrificial love of God?

In the Word

Read Matthew 27:27-44 together and discuss the following questions:

1. Crucifixion (hanging on a cross) was the Roman method of execution for slaves and foreigners. Generally, it took a long time for a

person to die, therefore making it excruciatingly painful. Death by crucifixion was unspeakably shameful and degrading, yet Jesus willingly suffered through the physical pain and humiliation in order for humankind to be set free from sin. After reading about the crucifixion of Jesus Christ, what are your impressions of Jesus?

2. Jesus was physically beaten and mocked before He was crucified. What do you imagine He was feeling—physically, emotionally and psychologically—during this ordeal of abuse?

3. Read Luke 23:26-43. What new insights do you gain from Luke's account?

4. Look again at Luke 23:39-43. What do you think Jesus meant when He said, "Today you will be with me in paradise" (v. 43)?

5. What implications does this conversation have for our lives?

6. Beyond Jesus' physical suffering, what did He bear in His death?

7. How was the death of Christ a sacrifice of love for you?

8. Because of His death, what are your benefits?

9. What is your response?

Reflect and Apply

1. If you were one of Jesus' disciples and you watched Him first being mocked and physically beaten, then struggling to carry the cross to Golgotha, and finally hanging on that cross, what thoughts would be going on in your mind?

2. How does the knowledge of Christ's suffering on the cross help you to understand the depth of His love for you?

3. Read 1 Peter 2:21-25. How does this Scripture help you better understand Christ's suffering for you?

4. What do you think verse 21 means?

5. Reread verse 24. How does this verse summarize the crucifixion of Jesus?

Spend a few minutes together in prayer as a family, thanking God for the sacrifice He made on your behalf.

51

The Death of Christ

Key Verses

With a loud cry, Jesus breathed his last. The curtain of the temple was torn in two from top to bottom. And when the centurion, who stood there in front of Jesus, heard his cry and saw how he died, he said, "Surely this man was the Son of God!"

MARK 15:37-39

The Big Idea

The death of Christ is the darkest moment in history, turned into the greatest demonstration of love and hope the world has ever known.

Focus

A medical doctor wrote the following about the physical pain that Jesus must have endured on the cross. Read this summary aloud and then discuss the question that follows. (Note: The following contains graphic descriptions that may not be suitable for younger kids.)

Like many others of His era, Jesus died on a cross by decree of Roman officials and endured one of man's most fierce tortures. But unlike others, He also bore the sins of the world on His sinless body—a spiritual agony we cannot begin to comprehend. We can, however, sense to a small degree His physical suffering.

Once in the tribunal area, the victim was stripped and his hands tied above his head to a supporting column. A soldier was stationed on each side of the condemned, and they took turns beating him with a flagrum—a short handle equipped with leather thongs whose ends were tipped with lead balls or sheep bones.

The thongs fell where they would, the leather strips burying themselves deep in the victim's body. When wrenched away, the lead balls ripped out bits of flesh. Hemorrhaging was intense, and the destruction of the condemned's body so extensive that even some Roman soldiers, hardened to brutality, were revolted.

National law prohibited more than 40 lashes. Ever cautious to uphold the law, Pharisees demanded the beatings be stopped at the thirty-ninth stroke. Rome had only one stipulation: The prisoner must remain alive and capable of carrying his crossbar to the execution.

Once the beating was completed, the near-naked victim was jerked to his feet, and the crossbar (weighing some 125 pounds) was laid on his shoulders. The condemned's arms were lashed to the crossbar, preventing a dash for freedom or striking out at his adversaries. A rope was commonly tied around his waist to direct his progress as he struggled through the streets. Romans preferred their victims naked; it was more humiliating. National preference, however, called for some clothing. The Romans usually agreed to this request by providing a loincloth.

Once the execution spot was reached, onlookers were held back and the victim was forced to the base of the stake. Then the crossbeam was removed from his back and experienced attendants threw him on the ground, grabbing his hands and stretching them out on the crossbar for size. The executioner placed an auger under each outstretched hand, and drilled a hole for the large crucifixion nail—a square spike about a third of an inch thick at its head.

The nail point was placed at the heel of the victim's hand. A single blow sent it ripping through the tissue, separating the carpal bones as it plunged into the crossbar. Paintings usually show the nail through the palm. Anatomically, this is impractical; the tissue cannot bear weight, and the victims would drop to the ground within minutes after being elevated.

Usually, the nail tore through the median nerve, creating an unending trail of fire up the victim's arms, augmenting the pain that tortured his body. From this moment on, this pain would intensify each time the victim moved, for the metal irritated the open nerve endings.

Once the victim was in place, the plaque that had preceded him was nailed to the crossbar, which was then elevated and, with a thud, dropped into place on the pointed stake.

Before the elevation, the condemned man's arms formed a 90-degree angle with his body. After elevation, the sag caused by the weight of an average man's body decreased this angle to 65 degrees, exerting a tremendous pull on each nail.

There was no need to nail the feet, but the guards were usually irritated by the inevitable flailing. To prevent this, they put one foot over the other and drove a nail through both. But this merely prolonged death.

If the Romans didn't nail the feet, the victim's body would hang on its arms, causing it to go into a spasm that prevented exhalation. The victim soon suffocated from an inability to use his respiratory muscles. The foot nail changed this. The urge to survive is ever present, even on the cross. It didn't take long for the crucified to discover he could exhale if he lifted himself on the nail in his feet. This was intensely painful, but the desire to breathe overcame the horror of the pain. This alternating lift and drop maneuver became a reflex action after a few hours. It could prolong life for as much as two days, depending on the individual's strength and determination. To this extent, the perpetuation of his life rested in the willpower of the crucified.

As the hours wore on, the victim's mental faculties were impaired. His body became soaked with sweat. Thirst became intense. Pain and shock were tremendous. This pathetic picture continued until the victim died.

Such was the horror of the crucifixion as Jesus dragged Himself from His knees in the Garden of Gethsemane to Golgotha. He had told His disciples—and this they could understand—that a man has no greater love than to lay down his life for his friends (see John 15:13). Before long they'd understand a love that surpasses even this—a love so divine that He laid down His life for His enemies as well.[1]

What emotions, feelings and thoughts came to your mind as you read this account of the crucifixion?

In the Word

Read Mark 15:33-47 together, and then discuss the following questions:

1. It is incredible how God took the darkest moment in world history and turned it into the greatest demonstration of love and hope the world has ever known. According to Mark 15:34, "Jesus cried out in a loud voice, 'My God, my God, why have you forsaken me?'" Why do you think He said that, and what did He mean by these words?

2. Why do you suppose the Roman centurion made the statement recorded in Mark 15:39: "Surely this man was the Son of God"?

3. What do you think the people in verse 40 might have been doing or talking about during the event?

4. Read John 3:16 and Romans 5:6-8. According to these Scriptures, what was the purpose of Christ's death on the cross?

5. "Justification" means "to be made right." Because of Christ's death, the believer in Christ can be made right with God—"just as if I'd never sinned." Read Romans 5:1. What is the result of being justified in Christ?

6. "Atonement" means "to cover or pardon." Your atonement as a believer means that your guilt and sin have been removed—Christ's death on the cross took the place of your spiritual death and set you free. In the Old Testament, the Day of Atonement was one of the major religious festivals of the year. Read Leviticus 16:29-34. What happened on this day, according to verse 30?

7. How often were the people's sins atoned for, or forgiven, according to verse 34?

8. Read 2 Corinthians 5:21 and 1 Peter 2:24. How is the death of Christ our atonement?

9. The New Testament form of atonement is *reconciliation*. Reconciliation means to change a person from an enemy to a friend. According to Colossians 1:19-22, how has the process of reconciliation taken place for you?

10. How does it make you feel knowing that Christ's physical death has reconciled you with God?

11. Which is a more meaningful symbol for you, the picture of Christ suffering on the cross before death or the picture of an empty cross with Christ resurrected? Why?

Reflect and Apply

1. Nearly 2,000 years ago in an obscure land, one Man died a common criminal's death on a cross. Yet that one Man's death has affected more lives than all of the other deaths before and after His. How has His death impacted the world?

2. According to 1 Peter 3:18, why did Christ die?

3. How does Ephesians 2:8-9 fit into this understanding of the death of Christ?

4. What can you do in order for the death of Christ to become relevant to your life?

5. Imagine yourselves at the funeral of Jesus of Nazareth. Your job is to, together, come up with the best words to describe the death and life of Jesus Christ. "Dearly Beloved, we are gathered together in the presence of God and the family and friends of our Master, Jesus of Nazareth . . ." What will your family's eulogy for Jesus be?

Note
1. Adapted from Edward R. Bloomquist, M.D., "No Guts, No Glory," *Breakaway* (April 1992), pp. 21-22.

The Resurrection

Key Verses

The angel said to the women, "Do not be afraid, for I know that you are looking for Jesus, who was crucified. He is not here; he has risen, just as he said."

MATTHEW 28:5-6

The Big Idea

The truth and power of Jesus Christ's victory over sin and death are based on His resurrection.

Focus

The resurrection of Jesus is the best news ever presented to humankind. Because of the Resurrection, we have life eternal and life abundant on earth. Begin today's challenge by imagining that an intelligent group of people from a remote part of the earth has just been discovered. Your job as a family is to tell them about the resurrection of Jesus and what it means to their eternal lives. What would you say? How would you describe Jesus' sacrifice to people who have never heard of Jesus?

In the Word

Now get into the Word and discuss the following questions together:

1. Read John 20:1-8. How would you summarize the events that occurred in this passage?

2. Read 1 Corinthians 15:17-19. What does Paul say about the resurrection in this passage?

3. If Jesus actually rose from the dead on the third day, what significance should that have for your faith?

4. What hope does the resurrection give you personally?

5. Read John 11:25-26. How does Jesus' statement deal with the impact of the resurrection on your life?

6. In order to believe in the resurrection of Jesus, you don't have to commit "intellectual suicide." There are a number of facts that are unexplainable if Jesus did not rise from the dead. For instance, Jesus foretold His resurrection. Read Matthew 16:21 and 17:22-23. Why were the disciples distressed by the words of Jesus?

7. The testimony of eyewitnesses and the transformation of the disciples can be explained logically only by the resurrection appearances of Jesus. Read 1 Corinthians 15:3-8. To whom did Jesus appear after He was raised from the dead?

8. The resurrection is the only explanation for the empty tomb. Read Mark 15:46 and Matthew 27:62-66. What were the precautions taken, both by the friends of Jesus and by His enemies, to ensure that His body would not be stolen?

9. The resurrection is the reason for the beginning of the Church and its rapid growth. Within a very short time period, the Christian faith spread all over the Roman Empire and beyond. What was the main subject of Peter's sermon found in Acts 2:29-32? What was the response of Peter's audience, according to Acts 2:37-42?

Reflect and Apply

1. Listed on the next page are the most common theories that skeptics throughout history have used to deny the resurrection. Read each of these statements and then, using the Scriptures you have looked at in this chapter, show the fallacy of these theories.

- The disciples stole Jesus' body and hid it.
- The Roman or Jewish authorities took Jesus' body.
- Jesus never died. He walked out of the tomb.
- The women and the disciples went to the wrong tomb.
- The disciples were hallucinating when they thought they saw Jesus risen from the dead.

2. How does the resurrection of Jesus separate Christianity from other religions?

3. Why do you think people deny Christianity even after hearing of the resurrection?

4. If the resurrection was a hoax, how would that affect your faith?

5. How can the resurrection of Jesus affect your life today?

6. What will you do differently because you know the power of His resurrection?

7. How can you use the resurrection power of Jesus to help your family live out the Christian life?

ACKNOWLEDGMENTS

Thanks and Thanks Again!

This book has my name on the cover, but as with all of my books, projects and ministry outreaches, there is a solid foundation of people who have played a major part in making it a reality. These faith conversations for families are part of a fresh movement of God to bring healthy spiritual legacy conversations back into the home, and I am privileged to have so many who support these efforts. I am a man most blessed.

Thank you especially to . . .

Cathy Burns: Our partnership in life and ministry is a remarkable gift. "Find a good spouse, you find a good life—and even more: the favor of God" (Proverbs 18:22, *THE MESSAGE*).

Christy, Rebecca and Heidi Burns: You are the reasons I am passionate about this material. You bring me more joy and love than a person can imagine.

Cindy Ward: Your life, authenticity, faith, ministry and amazing work ethic make all of this possible. I am eternally grateful for you.

Rod and Pam Emery: Your incredible leadership, dedication and generosity inspire me daily and have carried us through some difficult times without skipping a beat in ministry outreach.

Randy Bramel, Bucky Oltmans, Tom Purcell and Terry Hartshorn: I look forward to our weekly Tuesday morning times together. How fortunate I am to have a group of men to meet with who are also mentors, heroes, friends and role models.

Jon Wallace: I sometimes wonder if you realize all the good you do and how influential you are to this world. If you ever doubt, just know that

I admire you and respect you as much as any human being. Thank you for all that you do to make a difference.

Katie Norman: Your friendship and generous support over the years mean more than you will ever imagine. Your involvement with Home-Word's Creating a Media Safe Home initiative has multiplied more than we ever hoped. Bless you.

Aly Hawkins and Mark Weising: You did a superb job with editing this manuscript. You are the best.

HomeWord Staff and Board: Frankly, it is pretty amazing what God can do with such a committed staff and board who serve so faithfully and with so much inspiration.

Azusa Pacific University: I will invest the rest of my life working along-side the HomeWord Center for Youth and Family. Thanks especially to David Peck, Jon Wallace and Dave Bixby for making things happen.

HomeWord Donors: Your gifts large and small are an investment in the lives of families around the world. I am humbled by your generosity and ever so grateful for your support.

HOME HW WORD

WHERE PARENTS GET REAL ANSWERS

Get Equipped with HomeWord...

LISTEN
HomeWord Radio
programs reach over 800 communities nationwide with *HomeWord with Jim Burns* – a daily ½ hour interview feature, *HomeWord Snapshots* – a daily 1 minute family drama, and *HomeWord this Week* – a ½ hour weekend edition of the daily program, and our one-hour program.

CLICK
HomeWord.com
provides advice and resources to millions of visitors each year. A truly interactive website, HomeWord.com provides access to parent newsletter, Q&As, online broadcasts, tip sheets, our online store and more.

READ
HomeWord Resources
parent newsletters, equip families and Churches worldwide with practical Q&As, online broadcasts, tip sheets, our online store and more. Many of these resources are also packaged digitally to meet the needs of today's busy parents.

ATTEND
HomeWord Events
Understanding Your Teenager, Building Healthy Morals & Values, Generation 2 Generation and Refreshing Your Marriage are held in over 100 communities nationwide each year. HomeWord events educate and encourage parents while providing answers to life's most pressing parenting and family questions.

A Ministry with *Jim Burns*

In response to the overwhelming needs of parents and families, Jim Burns founded HomeWord in 1985. HomeWord, a Christian organization, equips and encourages parents, families, and churches worldwide.

Find Out More
Sign up for our FREE daily e-devotional and parent e-newsletter at HomeWord.com, or call 800.397.9725.

HomeWord.com

Small Group Curriculum Kits

Confident Parenting Kit

This is a must-have resource for today's family! Let Jim Burns help you to tackle overcrowded lives, negative family patterns, while creating a grace-filled home and raising kids who love God and themselves.

Kit contains:
- 6 sessions on DVD featuring Dr. Jim Burns
- CD with reproducible small group leader's guide and participant guides
- poster, bulletin insert, and more

Creating an Intimate Marriage Kit

Dr. Jim Burns wants every couple to experience a marriage filled with A.W.E.: affection, warmth, and encouragement. He shows husbands and wives how to make their marriage a priority as they discover ways to repair the past, communicate and resolve conflict, refresh their marriage spiritually, and more!

Kit contains:
- 6 sessions on DVD featuring Dr. Jim Burns
- CD with reproducible small group leader's guide and participant guides
- poster, bulletin insert, and more

Parenting Teenagers for Positive Results

This popular resource is designed for small groups and Sunday schools. The DVD features real family situations played out in humorous family vignettes followed by words of wisdom by youth and family expert, Jim Burns, Ph.D.

Kit contains:
- 6 sessions on DVD featuring Dr. Jim Burns
- CD with reproducible small group leader's guide and participant guides
- poster, bulletin insert, and more

Teaching Your Children Healthy Sexuality Kit

Trusted family authority Dr. Jim Burns outlines a simple and practical guide for parents on how to develop in their children a healthy perspective regarding their bodies and sexuality. Promotes godly values about sex and relationships.

Kit contains:
- 6 sessions on DVD featuring Dr. Jim Burns
- CD with reproducible small group leader's guide and participant guides
- poster, bulletin insert, and more

Parent and Family Resources from HomeWord for you and your kids...

One Life Kit

Your kids only have one life – help them discover the greatest adventure life has to offer! 50 fresh devotional readings that cover many of the major issues of life and faith your kids are wrestling with such as sex, family relationships, trusting God, worry, fatigue and daily surrender. And it's perfect for you and your kids to do together!

Addicted to God Kit

Is your kids' time absorbed by MySpace, text messaging and hanging out at the mall? This devotional will challenge them to adopt thankfulness, make the most of their days and never settle for mediocrity! Fifty days in the Scripture is bound to change your kids' lives forever.

Devotions on the Run Kit

These devotionals are short, simple, and spiritual. They will encourage you to take action in your walk with God. Each study stays in your heart throughout the day, providing direction and clarity when it is most needed.

90 Days Through the New Testament Kit

Downloadable devotional. Author Jim Burns put together a Bible study devotional program for himself to follow, one that would take him through the New Testament in three months. His simple plan was so powerful that he was called to share it with others. A top seller!

Small Group Curriculum Kits

Confirming Your Faith Kit

Rite-of-Passage curriculum empowers youth to make wise decisions...to choose Christ. Help them take ownership of their faith! Lead them to do this by experiencing a vital Christian lifestyle.

Kit contains:
- 13 engaging lessons
- Ideas for retreats and special Celebration
- Solid foundational Bible concepts
- 1 leaders guide and 6 student journals (booklets)

10 Building Blocks Kit

Learn to live, laugh, love, and play together as a family. When you learn the 10 essential principles for creating a happy, close-knit household, you'll discover a family that shines with love for God and one another! Use this curriculum to help equip families in your church.

Kit contains:
- 10 sessions on DVD featuring Dr. Jim Burns
- CD with reproducible small group leader's guide and participant guides
- poster and bulletin insert
- 10 Building Blocks book

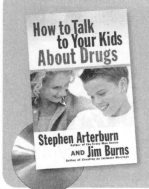

How to Talk to Your Kids About Drugs Kit

Dr. Jim Burns speaks to parents about the important topic of talking to their kids about drugs. You'll find everything you need to help parents learn and implement a plan for drug-proofing their kids.

Kit contains:
- 2 session DVD featuring family expert Dr. Jim Burns
- CD with reproducible small group leader's guide and participant guides
- poster, bulletin insert, and more
- How to Talk to Your Kids About Drugs book

Tons of helpful resources for youth workers, parents and youth. Visit our online store at www.HomeWord.com or call us at 800-397-9725

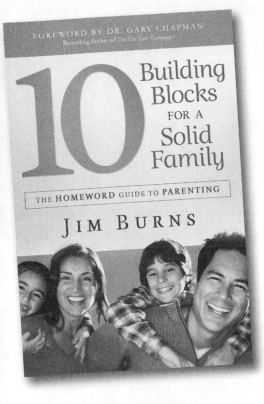